# EPISTEMIC DISSONANCE

## THE (R)EXISTENCE OF BLACK TRAVESTIS AND TRANS WOMEN IN BRAZIL

Edited by:
Megg Rayara G. de Oliveira,
Letícia Carolina Nascimento,
Jaqueline Gomes De Jesus

**Foreword by:**
M. Myrta Leslie Santana

**Afterword by:**
Rinaldo Walcott

**Translation organized by:**
Feibriss Ametista H. M. Cassilhas

AMÉFRICA
PRESS

Copyright © 2025 Megg Rayara G. de Oliveira, Letícia Carolina Nascimento, Jaqueline Gomes de Jesus Front cover image inspired by the artwork of Megg Rayara G. de Oliveira

All Rights Reserved. No part of this publication may be reproduced, distributed, or transmitted in any form or by any means, including photocopying, recording, or other electronic or mechanical methods, without the prior written permission of the publisher, except in the case of brief quotations embodied in critical reviews and certain other noncommercial uses permitted by copyright law. For permission requests, write to the publisher at the address below.

ISBN: 979-8-9872776-4-5
ISBN: 979-8-9872776-5-2

First English Translation Printed Edition 2025
Améfrica Press
P.O. Box 24647
Baltimore, MD 21214 USA
www.amefricapress.com

First Published in Portuguese in Salvador, BA: Devires, 2022 as:
Gritarias Epistêmicas: [r] existência de travestis e mulheres transexuais negras no Brasil

Edited by: Megg Rayara G. de Oliveira, Letícia Carolina Nascimento and Jaqueline Gomes de Jesus

Translation Organized by Feibriss Ametista Henrique Meneghelli Cassilhas

This is an authorized translation from the Portuguese language edition published by Editora Devires

ORGANIZAÇÃO
Megg Rayara Gomes de Oliveira
Letícia Carolina Nascimento
Jaqueline Gomes de Jesus

# GRITARIAS EPISTÊMICAS

## (r) existências de travestis e mulheres transexuais negras no Brasil

# We dedicate this book to Professor Fran Demétrio.

Este livro é dedicado à
professora doutora Fran Demétrio

Fran Demétrio was an Associate Professor in the Interdisciplinary Undergrad Program in Health (BIS) at the Health Sciences Center of the Federal University of Recôncavo da Bahia (UFRB) and a Permanent Professor in the Professional Master's Program in Family Health at FIOCRUZ (MPROFSAUDE/FIOCRUZ). She carved a brilliant path in academia—a postdoctoral degree in Philosophy from the University of Brasília, a Ph.D. in Public Health from the Institute of Collective Health at the Federal University of Bahia, a Master's degree in Food, Human Nutrition, and Health from the School of Nutrition Science from the Federal University of Bahia (ENUFBA), and a Bachelor's degree in Human Nutrition from ENUFBA.

Some of the main themes of her life-long research were humanization, comprehensiveness, and intersectionality in the areas of care, health and human nutrition; gender and sexuality; expanded clinical nutrition; quality of life; rationalities in health and human nutrition; breastfeeding; maternal and child nutrition; nutritional and sanitary epistemology; food security; interdisciplinary health education; and epistemic human rights.

In addition to her outstanding career as a scholar, Fran Demétrio was also significantly involved in the social movement of travestis and transgender people.

**Translated by Jess Oliveira**

# CONTENTS

Editor's Note .................................................................................................i

Translator's Note ..........................................................................................v

Foreword by M. Myrta Leslie Santana, PhD ..................................................xiii

Preface by Megg Rayara Gomes de Oliveira, Jaqueline Gomes de Jesus and Letícia Carolina Nascimento ...................................................................xvii

## PART I: The Testimonio and Research of Black Travestis and Transsexual Women ........................................................................ 1

**1 |** Black Travestis: Midwives of the Lgbt Movement by Jovanna Cardoso da Silva and Letícia Carolina Nascimento............................................ 2

**2 |** Who Cares About the Solidao of Black Transgender Women from the Periphery? by Ariane Moreira de Senna................................. 13

**3 |** Turning Holy into Dangerous: Transfeminine Bodies, Representation, and Erasures in the Visual Arts by the 19th Century by Megg Rayara Gomes de Oliveira ............................................................................................ 20

**4 |** Candomble: A Place of Resistance and Struggle for Citizenship and Religious Freedom for Trans Women and Travestis by Fernanda de Moraes da Silva................................................................................................ 56

**5 |** Quilombo Mandata: Black Travestis Disputing Political Institutionality by Erica Malunguinho and Maria Clara Araújo dos Passos ........................ 70

**6 |** Dandara, Marielle, and the Killability Politics in Brazil by Megg Rayara Gomes de Oliveira .................................................................................. 84

**7 |** Living Is the Art and Science of Resistance: A Conversation Between Jaqueline Gomes de Jesus and Rosa Luz ................................................ 90

**8 |** The Body: The Disabled Travesti by Luana Rayalla ................................ 105

## PART II: The Voices of Black Travestis and Trans Women in Social Media ................................................................................................ 109

**9 |** Cis'coloniality and the Transphobia Imaginary by Thiffany Odara ............ 110

**10 |** Can a Black Travesti Work in Social Work? by Jessyka Rodrigues ........... 115

11 | "Between Us Sistas": For an Abolitionist Anti-Racist Transfeminism by Dora Santana .................................................................................117

12 | LGBT Representation by Jaqueline Gomes de Jesus ...................122

13 | Brazilians Owe a Historical Debt to Travestis by Maria Clara Araújo dos Passos .........................................................................................125

14 | Pedagogy Of The Razor Blade And Molotov by Ayra Cristina Sousa Dias .................................................................................................129

15 | What Does It Mean to Have So Many Sources of Oppression in a Single Body During the Lockdown? by Carolina Iara de Oliveira ...................132

16 | Travesti Identity: Language Dispute and Redefinition by Dandara Maria Americano da Silva............................................................................141

17 | The Challenge of Being a Travesti Teacher Under the Bolsonaro Government by Ana Flor Fernandes Rodrigues......................................143

18 | Transphobia Is Structural and Our Children Are Taught to Exploit Hatred by Dália Celeste ..........................................................................147

19 | The Stressful Place of the Black Travesti Who Produces Academic Knowledge by Carolina Iara de Oliveira ..........................................151

20 | As Long as There Is Strength in This Black Transfemininity, I Will Go On: The Challenges of a Marked Body and Tensions Amidst the Covid-19 Pandemic in My Undergraduate Thesis by Joane Victória Viana Bastos .................................................................................................................155

21 | The Privilege to Work by Ayra Cristina Sousa Dias ....................160

22 | Black Travestis and Transgenders: Reverence to Strong Roots by Yara Canta ...........................................................................................163

23 | What is a Travesti Aquilombamento Capable Of? by Leticia Carolina Nascimento ... ..............................................................................166

Afterword: Dissonance Is Life; Or How We Might All Live Queer Lives by Rinaldo Walcott..........................................................................168

Translator Bios ..........................................................................172

# EDITOR'S NOTE

**Epistemic Dissonance** is one of the first, if not the first, book in English written by Brazilian Transwomen *and* Travesti. This groundbreaking book is a timely intervention into the field of Transgender Studies. Much like Feminist Studies, Women's Studies, Black Studies, and Gender studies, Transgender Studies is a field of inquiry that emerged outside of the academy, outside of universities. Because of the intellectual force that the field made outside of the academy, answering questions and, most importantly, naming existences, identities, and social phenomenon that the traditional fields of academic study did not have the tools to address, Transgender studies is now an emergent field of academic inquiry in the very institutions that defined trans* people as less than human.

This is a powerful anthology considering the moment in which it is being published. For decades in Brazil, trans*, queer and feminist activists have fought a well-funded retrogressive social movement that challenged what it called "gender ideology." Through cultivating a successful playbook that sought to undermine the progress of social groups defined as "leftist" in Brazil, this transnational movement has now emerged in the U.S. as an organized political force.

**Epistemic Dissonance** is a compilation of academic works, blogs, manifestos of (re)existence, and social media posts that reflect Brazilian transfeminist and travesti thought, much of which was written during the COVID-19 pandemic. This book is not just about Brazil, as Brazil is another country here in the Americas. All of the countries in the Americas are profoundly interconnected culturally, historically, politically, and economically, despite our linguistic differences. This is not to say that we are all the same. But it is a call to recognize how our differences both accentuate points of connection and points of possibility. We can learn from each other.

In this anthology, the reader will find some common ground in experiences that will resonate on a deep emotional level. The texts range from being vicarial, eye-opening, difficult, as well as downright beautiful. What I hope the reader will take away are new possibilities of thinking about gender and trans*ness. The profound interventions that are being made in gender studies in Latin America largely go ignored by English-speaking audiences, to our detriment. Take, for example, the gender category of travesti. Many of us in the U.S. and Canada are comfortable with using traditional European terms to describe various forms of gendered embodiment. We do not consider terms naming gendered existences that pertain to this hemisphere, to its history, and cultural variations. This approach ignores the Afro-Indigenous roots of the Americas.

Yes, this book centers the experiences of Black Transwomen and Travestis. However, it is important to note that when a book centers the diversity of Black folks, we center everyone. There are essays written by Disability activists, Intersex persons, working-class folks, middle-class, and upper-middle-class folks who question their class positionality. The reader will encounter terms that are without an English translation, because they point to a feeling, an existence that is experienced but not yet named or theorized in English. Some examples are *solidão*, (re)exist and (re)existence. The book engages more well-known theories from the Hemisphere, such as coloniality and the coloniality of being. The book, for many, will be an introduction to these terms. For others, it will be a very interesting rethinking and application of these concepts. In both cases, this book offers language that will be useful to those outside of Brazil, in naming many experiences that we feel, but simply do not have the words to name. We invite the reader to learn more about the concepts and ideas that are commonly used in a Brazilian context. We have offered footnotes for some key ideas for context, but the footnotes are not exhaustive.

In the following Translator Note, the translator offers her thoughts on the process of translation. So, I will leave much of that conversation to her. However, as the editor-in-chief of Améfrica Press, I would like the reader to note several important things: We treated each of the texts as individual stand-alone texts. Following the original book, we did not impose one style of writing across the texts but made sure that the style of writing in each text was consistent; this is particularly important for the Blog and Instagram posts that use a very informal language. That said, most of the texts do follow ABNT (The Brazilian Association of Technical Standards). The reader will also notice changes in style across each text. Some essays will use very informal language, as if you were talking to a person on the street. There are a lot of run-on sentences and other non-normative, dare I say, "illegitimate" forms of writing. Given the intervention that this book is making, this is kind of the point of some of the essays. Thus, in the overall anthology, the diverse writing style, diverse modes of academic citation are also an intentional move to reflect the diversity of voices and experiences of the authors.

We thank the Brazilian publisher Editora Devires, and most importantly, the authors, editors, and translators of this volume. This collection is a work of love and honesty. We hope that we were able to reflect these feelings in the translation. Translation is an approximation, but that is not the only goal, not for Améfrica Press at least. The goal, for us at Améfrica Press, is to open doors, to create connections, and to start/support conversations across linguistic and geopolitical boundaries.

So, we present this important anthology to you, the reader, with lots of love and strength, especially in this complicated moment that we are all facing across the world, especially here in the Americas.

Tanya L. Saunders
Editor-in-chief
Baltimore, MD
July 16, 2025

# TRANSLATOR'S NOTE

> "*Navalha debaixo da língua*
> *Tô pronta pra briga*
> *Navalha debaixo da língua*[1]
> *Somebody's gonna have to tell the truth and*
> *I'm gonna tell it!*"
> **Extract from the song Diaba by Urias (2019)**

Probably the first act of translation the reader will encounter in **Epistemic Dissonance: The (R)existence of Black Travestis and Trans Women in Brazil** is the bright red cover with a razor blade on the tongue[2]. A symbol that crosses borders. In Brazil, when associated with Black travestis and trans women, it tells us stories not everyone is aware of, even if they can make connections between those trans feminine existences, and the little deadly silver object easily available in local drugstores. The story has been told among academics, and in this context, it is told through the perspectives of people who are not trans, like Luiz Mott and Aroldo Assunção (1987), who conducted ethnographic research using interviews with travestis. Today, as this book illustrates, there is a notable increase in our presence in universities, especially because of Affirmative Action. Two travestis who are also authors of this book, Leticia Nascimento and Jessyca Rodrigues (2021),

---

[1] Razor blade under my tongue/ I'm ready to fight/ Razor blade under my tongue (my translation).

[2] The art on the cover is an AI version of the art by Megg Rayara Gomes de Oliveira made for the Brazilian edition.

alongside Rafael Meneses and Valdenia Araújo, reveal that the blade — often viewed as a symbol reinforcing the stereotype of travestis as aggressive — was frequently used by them to inflict harm on themselves. This behavior stemmed from their immediate association with HIV/AIDS, another stereotype, which led others, especially the police, to avoid them out of fear of infection. By understanding society's perceptions, they would use these stereotypes as a means of self-protection, illustrating a painful choice: opting for one form of suffering over another.

The mouth, illustrated on the cover wide open, holds not only a blade, but sharp words, and our vibrant (r)existence is one that has always been vocal, creating a dissonance for those who are unaccustomed or unwilling to listen to us. Regardless of how much sense we make or whether we are simply speaking to survive and advocate for our rights and protect our sisters, for those who don't understand our need to make noise to be heard, it must seem unpleasant and overwhelming to hear all our epistemics together. Our open mouths clearly convey the truth that our bodies — whether walking the streets or being forced out of our homes — assert our existence. We have always existed, and there is nothing wrong with us. On the contrary, we possess a power and knowledge that is vital for the entire community, even if they have forgotten it or cling to conservative narratives rooted in a colonial project that vilifies us. These narratives aim to erase our identities, stifle our spirits, and incite such hatred that we could be killed simply for existing.

There is a numerous blend of words frequently used among Black Brazilian scholars, artists, and activists, combining the meanings of resist and exist, and in this book's title, their choice was to spell it (r)existence. It is important to acknowledge, however, that all those variants trace back to the foundational thesis of Professor Ana Lúcia Silva Souza, published in 2011 and later translated into English by América Press in 2024 as *We're an Example of Trajectories and Victories": Hip Hop, Education and Literacies of Reexistence*. Reexistence is central to the concept of literacies of reexistence, which emphasizes the agency of the hip-hop movement literacy, which has a lot in common with the educational experiences of previous groups from the Black movement and its literacy practice. Since Dr. Souza's concept recognizes that knowledge does not come only from formal schooling, the diversity of texts and authors from different backgrounds in this collection contributes to expanding her creative method in the existence and writing of Black travestis and trans women.

This translation project, which I had the joy and honor of coordinating, took into account the ethical framework of the book itself. It aims to share knowledge without hierarchies by publishing academic articles, blog posts, and social media posts alongside each other. This approach is particularly important because many of us have endured violent experiences in educational settings, often leaving school without fully concluding our studies or learning as much as we could, due to the struggles of dealing with transphobia and racism. However, this does not mean that we are not producing knowledge. On the contrary, the travestis and transsexual movements have their roots in the streets. Drawing inspiration from this, I invited translators with diverse backgrounds and varying levels of experience, most of whom are Black and part of the LGBTQIA+ community, along with some allies.

Aline Silva Santos and Kenai dos Santos Roriz are students at the Federal University of Bahia (UFBA) who attended my classes, and they both exhibited a genuine personal and academic interest in these topics. Nathalia Amaya Borges is also a student who participates in my study group, Corsciência (my translation of "color consciousness" in Portuguese). This group focuses on being the color brave in our translations and storytelling practices. Kukua Dada is studying pedagogy at UFBA, has started working as a translator for websites, and is keen to learn translation from an academic standpoint. And because of that, we decided to collaborate on translating some texts in this book. I had the opportunity not only to work as a translator but also as a mentor to some beginner translators on the specificities and challenges of this field. One of the most important lessons I believe can be learned is the value of collaboration—not only discovering our own potential but also recognizing the potential in others. This can be challenging, but it highlights the tremendous value and outcomes that can arise from collective translation efforts.

Flávia Kunsch has been my translation partner since our time in the Master's program in Translation Studies at the Federal University of Santa Catarina (UFSC). I am a huge fan of her work and her perspective on languages, making it an easy decision to continue our partnership. Ale Mujica Rodriguez and Ti Ochoa are two academics who were part of the same group of trans activists as me at UFSC. They work professionally in translation and have made significant contributions to the trans community in their respective fields of study: Medicine and English. Bruna Barros and Jess Oliveira are part of the América Press translation team and are members of the same study group as I am: the Translating in the Black Atlantic collective at UFBA, coordinated by Professor Denise Carrascosa. They are also known as Cocoruto Art Duo, which is dedicated to co-translation, co-writing, and audiovisual experimentation.

Even though I coordinated this translation project, and Tanya Saunders reviewed it so that we could work together to ensure coherence among the translated works, we also made it a priority to consider that each translator's style should be taken into consideration. This reflects the nature of the book translated, which resonates with many voices, each with its own potential. One of our main concerns and interests in translating this book was to share with an English-speaking audience the work we, as Black travestis and trans Women, are producing in Brazil about our stories, struggles, and demands. To achieve that understanding, it's crucial to address the translation of the term "travesti."

It is widely recognized in various circles of artists, activism, and gender studies that the term "travesti" should not be translated. Using words like "transvestite" is a common mistake, often perpetuated by machine translation tools like Google Translate. In a message to the Black travesti and singer Linn da Quebrada, Black travesti and pedagogue Maria Clara Araujo—who also has a text in this book—explains to her friend why she believes "travesti" should remain untranslated, emphasizing the unique cultural and social significance of the term within our community.

> Friend, travesti is a Latin American identity, and to say this means that the particularities and the specificities of being a Brazilian travesti turn this identity into something unique worldwide. [...] The term travesti is not just a term; it carries a symbology, a representation, a social role, and a specific social place in Brazil. So, if we translate it, I'm afraid that it would take all the historicity of the travesti movement in Brazil, including that of having reclaimed a term that was used in a pejorative way for years, and re-signified it (ARAUJO, 2017)[3].

Araujo's point resonates with many activists in Brazil, who relate the travesti identity to similar identities around the world, such as the Mahus in Hawaii, Muxes in Mexico, Hijras in India, and Fa'afafine in Samoa. These groups are often considered part of a third gender in Western understandings of gender.

Developing this idea of the untranslatability of "travesti," artist, writer, macumbeira[4], and psychologist Castiel Vitorino Brasileiro argues that "*Travesti*

---

[3] [E.N.] please note that citations that to not have a page number are quotes from blogs or social media posts, which are cited in the reference section.

[4] [E.N.] this could be translated as "witch," but in the most pejorative sense of the term. The term has been reclaimed by practitioners of African-based religious traditions, for whom this term is often used.

*is not translated, and travesti is already a translation. Being travesti and spirituality are colonial translations of our transmutations*" (2020, our translation). This perspective invites reflection on the colonial gaze directed at us. Thus, there must be a shift in approach, and it must come from you, dear reader, to recognize and embrace the idea of reading us as a translation.

Each translation in this book approaches the task in its own way. Frequently, the definition of "travesti" is incorporated into the text itself by the writers of the text in Portuguese, as many of the writers recognize the importance of reflecting on our existence by examining this term, its history, and its implications. In other cases, such as in the text "Candomblé: A Place of Resistance and Struggle for Citizenship and Religious Freedom for Trans Women and Travestis" by Fernanda de Moraes da Silva, the translator Bruna Barros chose to include a definition in a footnote:

> Travesti is a transfeminine identity in Brazil. See Barros, Bruna and Jess Oliveira. 2020. "Black Sapatão Translation Practices: Healing Ourselves a Word Choice at a Time." *Caribbean Review of Gender Studies*, Issue 14: 43–52. [T.N.]

By providing a brief definition that contextualizes "travesti" as a transfeminine identity from Brazil, Barros highlights for the reader that there are additional sources to deepen their understanding of the term. This approach makes it clear that there are existing texts discussing travestis, authored by translators who engage thoughtfully with this process and are aware of the related issues. I believe this footnote draws attention to the translator's work, showcasing that they contribute not only as the translator of this book but also as a translator with a rich background that is worth knowing.

I firmly believe we have fulfilled our role, both as the writers of the Brazilian texts and as the authors of the English translations. Our responsibility as translators has limits, and the process of translation of concepts, ideas, and thoughts must be understood also as a task for the reader, who will not be underestimated in this translation project. We invite you to reflect upon the complexities within the book. If you are puzzled by the differences in the translations and definitions of the word travesti, it is probably because you are trying to see us as equivalents and the same. We are a community, we have a word in common, travesti! But we also have the right to differ in our understanding of the term. Our experiences stem from various places — whether the streets, universities, or even platforms like Spotify. Sometimes our knowledge comes from marginalized voices, including those of incarcerated individuals, and at times it emerges from the struggle for basic needs, the expressions found in art, our thesis, poetry, plays, or conversations held in bars or a friend's house after enduring another act of violence. This is why I invite you all to appreciate the plurality of attempts to translate a term that is so dear and important to us. Rather than seeking a single "perfect" translation, recognize that each of these attempts complements the others instead of competing. Embracing this diversity enriches our understanding and deepens our connection to the term and its significance within our community.

In my classes, I am an advocate of translator's notes, and I share many of them with students. As a translator, I'm thrilled to read translators' notes and see that translators were considered worthy of being listened to and understood as people who have important things to say about the book they've just translated. It seems simple and obvious, but we are still struggling with publishing houses to be able to work with some dignity. That is why I want to take this space to celebrate the meaningful connections and relationships that were paved by our ancestors! We are thankful for all the conversations that we no longer need to have because people fought so hard to be heard, to be understood, and taken into consideration. We continue this process in many other spaces, but this book's translation was a space of learning in a way we could trust that things would be done the best way possible. I celebrate the opportunity to express myself in the first Translator's Note I have written for a book and share with you a small part of these behind-the-scenes thoughts and actions on the process of translating this incredible book I admire deeply. I know that when I translate, many others are writing through me, and countless voices will continue to speak, write, or even dance because of those translated words — because language encompasses far more than just words.

Dr. Feibriss Ametista Henrique Meneghelli Cassilhas
Assistant Professor
Federal University of Bahia
PHD in Translation Studies by the Federal University of Santa Catarina

## References

ARAÚJO, Maria Clara. Transcript (ENG): **"Travesti" não se traduz!** 2017. Notes on Travecacceleration is curated by Ode and commissioned by Cairo Clarke, LUX Curatorial Fellow 2020/21. Available at: https://lux.org.uk/wp-content/uploads/2021/05/Travesti-na%CC%83o-se-traduz-by-Maria-Clara-Arau%CC%81jo_Transcript_ENG.pdf. Last accessed March 3, 2025.

BRASILEIRO, Castiel Vitorino. **Ancestralidade sodomita, espiritualidade travesti.** *PISEAGRAMA*, Belo Horizonte, n. 14, p. 40-47, jul. 2020. Also see: https://piseagrama.org/artigos/ancestralidade-sodomita-espiritualidade-travesti/. Last accessed Monday, September 1, 2025, at 9:46 pm

Mott, L. e ASSUNÇÂO, A. **Gilete na carne: etnografia das automutilações dos travestis da Bahia.** Temas IMESC, Soc. Dir. Saúde, São Paulo, 4(1): 41-56, 1987.

RODRIGUES, Jessyka da Silva; NASCIMENTO, Letícia Carolina Pereira do; MENESES, Rafael Martins de; ARAÚJO, Valdenia Pinto de Sampaio. **Vidas Precárias de Travestis Negras: Uma Geografia do Machismo e da Transfobia em Parnaíba -PI.** Revista Latino Americana de Geografia e Gênero, v. 12, n. 2, p. 39-55, 2021. ISSN 2177-2886.

# FOREWORD

M. Myrta Leslie Santana[5], PhD
Associate Professor, UC San Diego
August 2025

It would be hard to overstate the significance and urgency of a collection like *Epistemic Dissonance* in times like these. Originally published in Brazil during the apocalyptic churning of both the COVID-19 pandemic and the presidency of the fascist authoritarian Jair Bolsonaro, the English translation of *Gritarias epistêmicas* is coming during a renewed moment of crisis, even as the intervening years were far from a reprieve. In the face of growing transnational transphobia, unchecked white supremacy, unhinged US imperialism, runaway global capitalism, persistent genocide, and the rising tide of fascism, the Black travestis and trans women whose writing graces the following pages demonstrate to us, as Leticia Carolina Nascimento says in the last piece in the book, what a travesti aquilombamento is capable of.

Throughout the collection, the authors offer a heterogeneous and inspired account of the violence that Black travestis and trans women endure, the constraints on their labor and dignity, and also—to be sure—their inexorable acts of resistance and pathbreaking contributions to expressive culture. Much of what I want to celebrate in this foreword is addressed in the editor's note, the translator's note, and the foreword to the

---

[5] M. Myrta Leslie Santana is an ethnomusicologist and performer whose work examines the social and political significance of trans and queer performance in the Americas. She is the author of *Transformismo: Performing Trans/Queer Cuba* (Michigan, 2025), an ethnography of drag performance in contemporary Cuba that documents the ways trans and queer performers on the island interact with intensifying racial, sexual, and economic inequity.

Brazilian edition, all of which deserve serious attention. However, I believe it bears repeating, and I will attempt to underscore further the importance of the interventions I understand *Epistemic Dissonance* to be making.

All of the front matter to *Epistemic Dissonance* emphasizes the hemispheric scope and vision of the collection, as well as its place within and relevance to the Americas as a whole. You can see this, for example, in the transnational citational universe discussed in the original foreword and present throughout the text. Or the creative deployments of the untranslated word "travesti" in distinct contexts. Take, as one case, the essay by Jovanna Cardoso da Silva and Letícia Carolina Nascimento in which they claim US Black and Latinx trans/queer icons Marsha P. Johnson and Sylvia Rivera as travestis. This fact, they tell us, is "not a historical incongruity. It is political recognition." And Johnson and Rivera are not alone: A few pages down, da Silva and Nascimento identify Audre Lorde as a "Black Latina-Caribbean feminist," and in an earlier essay, Megg Rayara Gomes de Oliviera identifies 19th-century New Yorker Mary Jones as a Black travesti sex worker.

This is all to say that the authors of *Epistemic Dissonance* make clear that they are not only proposing that these contents have hemispheric reach; they are insisting that these questions and histories are already and have always been interconnected across the fictions of national borders and language. I see this as a generous invitation to the new readers of the English language version to, as Tanya Saunders suggests in their editor's note, take the thinking of Black travesti and trans authors in Brazil and Latin America seriously. To not do so would not only extend the injustice of US cultural hegemony, but it would also foolishly debilitate the necessary strength of our transnational movements as we combat the global oppressions of this stultifying moment.

Another way to say this is that *Epistemic Dissonance* amplifies voices that are all but silenced in mainstream academic discourse, even in the allegedly non-normative spaces of trans and queer studies. You can see this throughout the text in the diverse deployments of terms like "periphery" and "margins" to describe the positions these authors wish to bring to the fore: the epistemologies of Brazil's peripheral neighborhoods, the peripheral place of entire nation-states in the global order, the marginalization of Black women in academia, the marginal nature of hip hop culture in Brazil, the marginalization of travestis. *Epistemic Dissonance* insists that these peripheries and margins have always been, and continue to be, key sites of incisive analysis.

One way the collection accomplishes this is through its varied and unflinching writerly voices. If, in scholarly discourses, thoughts that challenge hegemonic structures tend to be accommodated only insofar as they conform to the genteel norms of academic speech, the authors of *Epistemic Dissonance* refuse to bow their tongues to metrics of higher education. Though the ideas presented throughout the collection are as rigorous and insightful as any text can hope to be, they are offered in a language that meets the exigencies of the context from which they come rather than appeasing academia's hesitant appetite. Notice, for example, the liberal use of exclamation marks throughout, as though to shake the reader. Or the thoughtful deployment of personal narrative and experience to ground the book's interventions. Or the urgent, topical interventions of the shorter texts that make up the second part of the collection.

As a musician myself, perhaps I should close by reflecting briefly on the choice of "dissonance" in the English-language title. What does it mean to have or to be in epistemic dissonance? In music, dissonance can refer to unharmonious sounds of various sorts, from a note that is begging for resolution to an erroneous one to one that comes from an entirely different harmonic or timbral world than those around it. I hear the authors of *Epistemic Dissonance* residing especially in that final one, offering tantalizing, irresistible ways of knowing that emerge from a consciousness fundamentally distinct from the constant humming of global capitalism, US imperialism, white supremacy, and cis-heteropatriarchy.

Listen, for example, to Ayra Cristina Sousa Dias when she tells us that she has "adopted ... the pedagogy of the razor blade and Molotov." By this, she means: "I make statements that will be immediately heard, in what is usually understood as a harsh and aggressive way. From now on, I will be bitter and harsh, and whoever expects sweetness can make their own candy at home." If we listen and read carefully, perhaps we can find ways to harmonize with such a call, to drown out the suffocating din that conspires to forestall Black travesti and trans life and liberation. I don't know how you could read *Epistemic Dissonance* and not be moved to work toward the kinds of worlds imagined in its pages.

# PREFACE

**Megg Rayara Gomes de Oliveira
Jaqueline Gomes de Jesus
Letícia Carolina Nascimento
Translated by Feibriss Ametista Henrique Meneghelli
Cassilhas and Ti Ochoa**

Epistemic Dissonance: The (R)existence of Black Travestis and Trans Women in Brazil is a Special Publication by professors and researchers Jaqueline Gomes de Jesus (Federal Institute of Rio de Janeiro), Leticia Carolina Pereira do Nascimento (Federal University of Piauí), and Megg Rayara Gomes de Oliveira (Federal University of Paraná). It aims to highlight texts, academic or not, produced by Black travestis and trans women. These works intersect across ethnicity and race, gender, and sexual diversity, while engaging with the field of education in both formal and informal spaces.

However diverse, the texts included in Epistemic Dissonance are all critical of the silence that hovers over the experiences of Black travestis and trans women as researchers and as social and political subjects. We assume a position that allows analysis of numerous forms of exclusion and also multiple forms of resistance.

Our research confirms that Blackness in Brazil is constituted by heterosexual cisgender norms, disregarding other possibilities for constructing Black identities. Within this normative construction, sexualities considered deviant, such as homosexuality, bisexuality, pansexuality, and asexuality, as well as gender identities like transgender and travesti, would, to some extent, be seen as betrayals of one's racial identity.

Such attitudes, we find, are associated with several factors, notably the violent colonizing process that imposed white cisgender heterosexuality as the only possibility for bodies and sexuality. This process is also responsible for the low representation that travestis and trans women have in Black social movements, and for the reduced number of Black travestis and trans women working in institutions of higher education.

Ângela Figueiredo (2008) cautions that "gender and race studies often blur the lines between the subject and the object of investigation in gender and race studies" (FIGUEIREDO, 2008, p. 239, our translation) and that "the preference for certain themes is related both to the researcher's sexual orientation and gender identity, and to their sense of belonging to their racial group" (Megg Rayara Gomes de OLIVEIRA, 2017, p. 87, our translation). Therefore, it is possible to argue that the researchers' gaze would be directed by their subjectivities. In the case of Black travestis and trans women researchers, this gaze would come "from the periphery and the abysses" (HARAWAY, 1995, p. 22, our translation), or from the terrain of subjugated people (HARAWAY, 1995).

However, the perspectives of subjugated individuals should not be free from critical reassessment, decoding, deconstruction, and interpretation.

These positionings, Haraway reminds us (1995), are not "innocent." Black transgender and travesti women have broad experiences with modes of denial through repression, forgetting, and acts of disappearance—with ways of being nowhere while claiming to see everything. But subjugated people have a decent possibility of recognizing God's tricks and all his brilliant—and thus blinding—illumination (HARAWAY, 1995, p. 23). A type of illumination directed to bodies that matter and, therefore, deserve to be remembered.

Just as "the master's tools will never dismantle the master's house" (Audre Lorde, 1979), Black trans women and travestis need to use different strategies to light up the paths they tread in the process of constructing their own epistemologies: lighters, candles, lanterns, torches, bonfires, and everything at hand, so "the personal and the political can begin to illuminate all our choices" (LORDE, 1979).

Differences that occur in the social and political field: never [occur] in the field of biology!

Problematizing this issue demands action.

Actions led by Black travestis and trans women contribute, then, to closing social, political, and epistemic gaps and preventing the invisibility of those considered to be gender and race dissident.

Perhaps the hottest spark—one that ignites, warms, illuminates, and invites celebration around the campfire of the epistemologies constructed by Black travestis and trans women—is the concept of intersectionality. This idea was present in the reflections of lesbian and heterosexual cisgender Black intellectuals in the United States and Brazil during the 1970s and 1980s.

However, the wood feeding the bonfire that illuminates the way comes from different places, such as decolonial studies, studies of ethnic-racial and gender relations, transfeminist theory, and social movements organized by Black travestis and trans women. Life trajectories, combined with the theories indicated and the concept of intersectionality, make it possible to "understand narratives as a result of everyday practices, which, in turn, can be understood as historical and as denouncing of the rules that have produced and governed them" (Marcio CAETANO, 2016, p. 33, our translation). This makes it possible to also understand the resistances used by the subjects of this book, which, individually or in groups, question that governing.

The individual experiences of Black travestis and trans women, preserved in memory, may be a result of reflections updated by today's experiences. Furthermore, they may spark debate and highlight realities from various periods in the history of Brazil and the countries impacted by the African diaspora, thus confirming that "our footsteps come from afar" [6]. " The reconnection with the past, explains Muniz Sodré (1988), "it only occurs in the reconstruction of memory through a system of values that coincides with the present social framework, itself a stable and dominant memory [...], but open to the indeterminacy of reality" (SODRÉ, 1988, p. 85, our translation).

In the case of black transvestites and transsexual women, the current social situation places them in a situation of isolation, exclusion, violation of rights, physical and psychological violence, etc., permeated by stereotypical, reductionist, marginal views, which would authorize, to a certain extent, erasure, making it difficult to reconnect with the past and with ancestry.

An ancestrality "anchored in the body and in embodiment" (Edileuza Penha de SOUZA, our translation), therefore, without a direct relation to kinship or lineages.

We know that the words travesti and trans women, as we know them today, were consolidated in the second half of the 20th century, but the subjects to which they refer weren't. When we use the vocabularies of travesti and trans women, we don't ignore the fact that these terms don't designate a reality in and of themselves, but are people who are a "product" of the moral vocabulary of modernity (Adriana Nunan do Nascimento

---

[6] [E.N.] "Our footsteps come from afar" is a translation of the phrase "Nossos Passos Vêm de Longel." The phrase, popularized by Jurema Werneck, who is currently the Executive Director of Amnesty International in Brazil, in her article entitled: "Nossos Passos Vêm de Longe: O Ensino de História na Construção de uma Educação Antirracista e decolonial." (Our Steps Come from Afar: History Teaching in the Construction of an Anti-Racist and Decolonial Education), has become a mantra in Brazil. It is seen as a Black feminist statement that serves as a reminder that the journey towards social justice, and racial equality, is still long but that ancestral strength and wisdom are sources of inspiration and motivation.

SILVA, 2007, p. 17, our translation). They are concepts as historical and socially constructed as any others.

Thus, to identify them in historical periods that precede the use of these terms, we adopt a genealogical approach, as stated by Ines Dussel and Marcelo Caruso (2003), and we employ the partial perspective suggested by Donna Haraway (1995) to critically analyze fragments of traditional history.

Even though this publication was born out of the necessity to highlight theoretical production by Black travestis and trans women who are scholars, the path to its effectuation took other directions.

The bonfire of trans epistemologies ignited new pathways, guiding the organizers to the travesti and trans women's social movements and to social networks, where they found a myriad of narratives and texts suitable for this publication.

The adopted stance, then, was to address multiple knowledges, academic or not, in a horizontalized way, avoiding hierarchies.

The choice of authors and texts sought to highlight that the experiences and interests of black transvestites and transsexual women are multiple and plural.

The book, then, is divided into two parts: texts produced specifically for this publication, and texts [reproduced] from the internet. This division is only organizational and not hierarchical.

The initial section, EPISTEMIC DISSONANCE PART 1: THE TESTIMONIO AND RESEARCH OF BLACK TRAVESTIS AND TRANSSEXUAL WOMEN, is comprised of six scholarly articles by seven distinguished authors.

The article **Black Travestis: Midwives of the LGBT Movement** is co-written by one of the most important travesti leaders in the country, Jovanna Cardoso da Silva, and by a professor from the Federal University of Piauí, Letícia Carolina Pereira do Nascimento. This is not only a generational gathering, but also one of knowledge and epistemologies, proving that it is possible for the social movement of travestis and trans people and the academy to come closer in the process of knowledge production.

Ariane Moreira de Senna, a psychologist and graduate student in Ethnic and African Studies in the School of Philosophy and Human Sciences at the Federal University of Bahia (UFBA), asks: **Who cares about the solidão[7] of the Black transgender women from the periphery?**

The author warns that *solidão* goes way beyond the idea of marrying or the presence/absence of sexual and affective partners in Black travestis and trans women's lives. "It crosses all our life since childhood, or at least since the first moment we transition."

According to Megg Rayara Gomes de Oliveira in the article **Turning Holy into Dangerous: Transfeminine Bodies Representation and Erasures in the Visual Arts by the 19th Century**, even prior to the advent of writing, images were (and continue to be) used to spread specific

---

[7] [E.N.] in the WSQ Special Issue on Solidão (2021), the editors write, in their introduction, that *Solidão* as defined by Ana Cláudia Pacheco (2013) describes the affective marginalization of Black women and the exploitation, hypersexualization, and invisibility of Black women in larger society and in social institutions, including the family, which is constitutive of the subjectivities of Black women and as Black feminine subjects. They write: "There have been some critiques of the term *solidão* as being very heteronormative (centered on the experiences of Black women within heterosexual relationships and within traditional families). Our use of the term *solidão* is a form of disidentification; it is explicitly in conversation with the Black *bicha,* Black trans, Black nonbinary, Black lesbian, *sapatão,* Afro-Cuir, and the multiple Black gender- and sexual-dissidents who, in studying Black feminist conceptualizations of *solidão*, have applied the term to understand their becoming as nonnormative Black subjects. Disidentification is a negotiation; it's developed by minority subjects; it's made in order to survive and thrive; it is a deliberate act of *living* in a majoritarian public sphere without denying some aspect of oneself. It is a set of strategies and practices to not only defy normative citizenship, but to resignify it. Much like *solidão*, it is a living theory that emerged from shared affective traumas (18-19). See: RAMOS SILVA, Luciane; SAUNDERS, Tanya L.; OHMER, Sarah Soanirina (eds.). *Women's Studies Quarterly*. Special Issue on Solidão/Black Women's Affect. Women's Studies Quarterly, New York, v. 49, n. 1, 2021. P. 16–49. doi:10.1353/wsq.2021.0040.

ways of thinking that could be used to perpetuate, or question, power dynamics.

Based on this statement, the author takes a panoramic tour through the history of the visual arts, with the objective to contribute, even if in a modest way, to breaking with the relative invisibility of representations of travestis and trans women, white and Black, seeking to identify works and artists that portray travestis and trans women in different periods and cultures up to the 19th century.

Fernanda de Moraes da Silva, in the article **Candomblé: A Place of Resistance and Struggle for Citizenship and Religious Freedom for Trans Women and Travestis**, offers a brief literature review emphasizing the importance of travestis and trans women in the emergence, preservation, and dissemination of Afro-Brazilian religiosity. According to the author, the presence of travestis and trans women inside Candomblé Houses—including the main figure, Iyálòrísá (popularly called Mães-de-Santo), or as Ómó Òrísá (filhas-de-santo)—represents the strength of Candomblé as a religion while rescuing the Black transsexual identity in Brazil.

Erica Malunguinho and Maria Clara Araújo dos Passos' article **Quilombo Mandata: Black Travestis Disputing Political Institutionality**, emphasizes the importance of the Social Political Movement of Travestis and Trans Women and the Black Women's Movement. The authors discuss how the movement called Mandata Quilomba, based in São Paulo and led by State Deputy Erica Malunguinho, positions itself as a politically and pedagogically engaged project that injects alternative political, ethical, and epistemological propositions into the political culture of Brazil.

Based on the concept of necropolitics proposed by Achille Mbembe (2012), in the essay **Dandara, Marielle, and Killability Politics in Brazil**, Megg Rayara Gomes de Oliveira discusses how power in postcolonial times confined Marielle Franco and Dandara dos Santos to the terrain of generic brutality. They even foresaw their own deaths, for not fitting into the manipulative normativities of white cisheterosexuality.

The last chapter of Section One, **Living is the Art and Science of Resistance: A Conversation Between Jaqueline Gomes de Jesus and Rosa Luz**, as the title suggests, is a dialogue between a scientist and an artist. They simultaneously occupy the positions of interviewees, interviewers, and authors. As they explain, the interview/text (or the text/interview) is a self-reflection on paths of resistance across different generations. It is a dialogue between trans Black women.

The book's second section, EPISTEMIC DISSONANCE: PART II - THE VOICES OF BLACK TRAVESTIS AND TRANS WOMEN IN SOCIAL MEDIA, is made up of sixteen texts that address different themes, produced in many regions of the country, with one written in the United States of America. Unlike the articles that comprise the first part of this book, the texts in the second part are shorter, leaner, and more subjective than those in Part I—which does not mean that they are less profound.

Luanna Rayalla's essay **The Body: the Disabled Travesti** is situated at the intersection of gender and sexuality studies and disability studies.

The starting point of the debate, as proposed by Luana Rayalla, is the concept of beauty and how it operates to establish either rigid or flexible limits on the process of relationship building pertaining to affect, desire, and friendliness. Beauty is a fluid and multifaceted concept. When applied to different bodies without conformity to traditional norms, it can evoke good feelings, such as pleasure and desire.

Thiffany Odara also discusses affection, sociability, and rejection, but adds to the debate issues such as violence, the job market, adjustments, and resistance to certain gender norms when discussing **Cis'coloniality and the Transphobia Imaginary**, which is also the title of her essay.

Without any ceremony, she questions the authority of a Cis-tem, which unsuccessfully attempts to homogenize travestis and trans women's identities, demanding that they reframe their daily lives so that they do not fall into the traps imposed by cis-coloniality.

The question asked by Jessyka Rodrigues in **Can a Black Travesti Work in Social Work** debates issues that affect the daily life of a travesti student's experience in the university. Long-standing issues presumed settled, such as the right to use one's chosen name and pronouns based on one's gender identity, and access to female bathrooms, are debated again.

Even though the text narrates her personal experience, it dialogues with situations lived by numerous Black travestis and transexual women who access higher education because, as a rule, they are bodies marked by gender and race, understudied categories in academic spaces.

Dora Santana lives and works in the United States of America. Her text, **"Between Us Sistas": for an Abolitionist Anti-Racist Transfeminism**, fosters a critical exchange of reflections between the author herself and Black and white intellectuals/activists from both the USA and Brazil, about envisioning an abolitionist and anti-racist transfeminism as an anti-racist, anti-transphobic, and anti-CIS-temic theory and practice that can forge our freedom.

Issues that are not always easy, that involve **LGBT Representation** in institutions and political parties, as discussed by Jaqueline Gomes de Jesus, who draws attention to the limits of an inclusion that is merely symbolic, fragile, and structural. Her presentation brings visibility to segments of a historically discriminated (oppressed) social group, who affirm the unconscious bias of a dominant group that does not want to see itself as oppressive or unjust. The author also argues that superficial concessions do not serve the collective and only temporarily alleviate the feeling of guilt of those who hold power.

Maria Clara Araújo dos Passos adopts a provocative and accusatory tone in her essay, echoing that of Jaqueline Gomes de Jesus. She argues that **Brazilians Owe a Historical Debt to Travestis**.

Her narrative highlights both the lack of empathy shown by the Brazilian population towards travestis and, consequently, the difficulty in understanding their pain. It is as if travestis don't bleed!

Pain cannot be in vain: it must and can be transformed into theory, as bell hooks suggests.

Besides reflecting on the little concern about the pain lived by Brazilian travestis, Maria Clara provokes cis-allies to assume a position of reparation and not omit themselves in situations of violence committed against the travesti community. In an emphatic tone, she calls on cisgender people to create opportunities, to ensure the existence of, and the guarantee of, rights as well as the physical and psychological integrity of travestis, so that they experience wellbeing and safety among cisgender people.

In the text **Pedagogy of the Razor Blade and Molotov**, Ayra Cristina Souza Dias also condemns the violence that affects the travesti community and how their voices remain silenced, even among the LGBT movement.

The author calls attention to the didactic-pedagogic role that travestis play in society. However, when travestis access spaces of formal education as professors, they are constantly discredited.

Ayra proposes, as a coping strategy, the use of the "pedagogy of the razor blade and Molotov": making statements that are sometimes perceived as harsh or aggressive, but are immediately heard. In conclusion, she reasons: "I will be bitter and harsh, and whoever expects sweetness can make their own candy at home!"

In the text, **What Does It Mean to Have So Many Sources of Pppression in a Single Body During the Lockdown?** Carolina Iara de Oliveira shares her harrowing experiences to discuss the pandemic realities for transgender women and travestis, and raises the question: "How is it possible not to go mad with Bolsonaro's eugenics policies?"

Carolina Iara denounces the federal government's policy of death, which, in disdaining the coronavirus pandemic, scrapped health and education policies, and job and income generation, which increased the exclusion of the most vulnerable people.

While confined at her home in the city of São Paulo, Carolina Iara's vision transcends the walls of her yard, and a prophetic prediction emerges: "There are so many uncertainties. The rope tightens itself, and we are walking around on it, trying constantly to keep our balance."

It is evident that… others will continue to keep their balance as best as they can.

Maintaining balance to prevent falling is the reality for most Black Brazilian travestis who came before and continue to make our existence possible with their struggle. With our struggle! Beginning with the question "What is a travesti, or rather, what can a travesti do!?" Dandara Maria Americano da Silva discusses the numerous intersections, such as race and class, to discuss Brazilian trans identity in the text **Travesti Identity: Language Dispute and Redefinition**.

Ana Flor Fernandes Rodrigues also organizes her discussion around a question that has been with her for a while: "What if your kid's teacher were a travesti?" Without the intention of giving a final answer, Ana Flor discusses, in the text **The Challenge of Being a Travesti Teacher Under the Bolsonaro Government**, some issues that interfere with the didactic-pedagogical practices of travesti teachers, especially in the current political context.

Although Dália Celeste's text, entitled **Transphobia is Structural and Our Children Are Taught to Exploit Hatred**," does not discuss childhood; rather, it addresses the violence that affects the bodies of transgender women and travestis in the city of Recife, which is undoubtedly a result of a social pedagogy that not only tolerates but also teaches and encourages transphobic violence.

Carolina Iara de Oliveira, in the text **The Stressful Place of the Black Travesti Who Produces Academic Knowledge**, also discusses violence, but in academic contexts. She questions the supposed neutrality that characterizes the production of white, cisgender, and heterosexual researchers who, unconsciously, classify what is produced by travestis, especially by Black travestis, as militant. This scenario both undermines the validity of the issues raised by Black trans individuals in academic environments and causes them physical and psychological distress.

It is an illness that affects the Black transfeminine community indiscriminately, in all academic spaces.

A similar circumstance is described by author Joane Victória Viana Bastos in the text **As Long as There is Strength in This Black Transfemininity, I Will Go On: The Challenges of a Marked Body and Tensions Amidst the Covid-19 Pandemic During My Undergraduate Thesis**. The text narrates her journey as a trans Black student in a pedagogy course in a small town in the countryside of Minas Gerais, where she experienced numerous uncomfortable and repeated adversities. According to Joane, the university environment clearly was not made to welcome our bodies.

The formal job market environment is constantly changing but remains reticent to the presence of travestis and trans women, especially Black ones.

Ayra Cristina Sousa Dias states that the search for work is not an option for poor, Black, and gender-dissident people. In her text entitled **The Privilege to Work**, she narrates the difficulties she faces in being seen and treated as a professional. Her search for formal work, just like for most Black travestis and trans women, is hampered by transphobia and structural racism, which ends the few hiring possibilities, with the justification that, as a candidate, she doesn't have the "profile" the company is looking for.

Yara Canta celebrates Black trasvestis and transgender people's ancestry. She identifies and pays tribute to this ancestry within the social movement through her text **Black Travestis and Transgenders: A Reverence to Strong Roots**. Despite the obstacles and countless situations of violence, Yara is categorical when stating: "We break with the patterns imposed by whiteness, by the colonial and cissexist system that tries to kill us at every moment. We create life! We are the past, the present, and the future."

Black trans women's and travestis' fight, past and present, can be considered a quilombo. In **What is a Travesti Aquilombamento Capable of?** the question is answered without mincing words as she explained that, as a decolonial clinic, travesti quilombos can heal our wounds, because the welcoming happens with an exchange of glances, via a sensitive listening, with warming and caring words.

As a decolonial shelter, the travesti quilombos can be a place of hospitality, where the differences do not inferiorize us.

## References

CAETANO, Marcio. **Performatividades reguladas: heteronormatividades, narrativas biográficas e educação**. Curitiba: Appris, 2016.

CRENSHAW, Kimberlé. **Documento para o encontro de especialistas em aspectos da discriminação racial relativos ao gênero**. Translated by Liane Schneide. Rev. Estud. Fem., Florianópolis, v. 10, n. 1, p. 171- 188, jan. 2002.

DUSSEL, Inés; CARUSO, Marcelo. **A invenção da sala de aula: uma genealogia das formas de ensinar**. São Paulo: Moderna, 2003; p. 103 – 156.

FIGUEIREDO, Ângela. **Dialogando com os estudos de gênero e raça no Brasil**. In: OSMUNDO, Pinho; SANSONE, Livio (Orgs.). Raça: novas perspectivas antropológicas. 2. ed. Salvador: EDUFBA, 2008, p. 237-255.

HARAWAY, Donna. **Saberes localizados: a questão da ciência para o feminismo e o privilégio da perspectiva parcial**. Translated by Mariza Corrêa. Cadernos Pagu, n. 5, 1995, p.07-41.

LORDE, Audre. Mulheres negras: As ferramentas do mestre nunca irão desmantelar a casa do mestre (1979). Translated by tatiana nascimento. In: **Textos escolhidos de Audre Lorde. Difusão Herédita: edições lesbofeministas independentes**, 2012. Available at: https://we.riseup.net/assets/171382/AUDRE%20LORDE%20COLETANEA-bklt.pdf. Last access September 1, 2025 at 10:05 pm.

LORDE, Audre. The Master's Tools Will Never Dismantle the Master's House, in: Lorde, Audre. **Sister outsider: essays and speeches**. New York: The Crossing Press Feminist Series, 1984. 110-113.

MACEDO, José Rivair. **Jagas, Canibalismo e "Guerra Preta": os Mbangalas, entre o mito europeu e as realidades sociais da África Central do século XVII**. Revista História (São Paulo), v.32, n.1, p. 53-78, jan/jun 2013. ISSN 1980-4369

OLIVEIRA, Megg Rayara Gomes de. **O Diabo em forma de gente: (r)existência de gays afeminados, viados e bichas pretas na educação**. Dissertation (PHD in Education) - Federal University of Paraná, Curitiba, 2017.

SODRÉ, Muniz. **O terreiro e a cidade: a forma social negro-brasi- leira**. Petrópolis: Vozes,1988.

SOUZA, Edileusa Penha de. **A ancestralidade africana de Mestre Didi expandindo a intelectualidade negra Brasileira**, n.d. Available at: http://www.brasa.org/wordpress/Documents/BRASA_IX/Edileuza-Penha-de-Souza.pdf. Last accessed November 11, 2019.

SILVA, Adriana Nunan do Nascimento. **Homossexualidade e discriminação: o preconceito sexual internalizado**. Dissertation (PHD in Psychology) – Pontifícia Universidade Católica do Rio de Janeiro, Rio de Janeiro, 2007.

# PART I
# EPISTEMIC DISSONANCE:
## THE TESTIMONIO[8] AND RESEARCH OF BLACK TRAVESTIS AND TRANSSEXUAL WOMEN

---

[8] [E.N.] Testimonio is a form of testimonial narrative pioneered by the Cuban Anthropologist Miguel Barnet. In this title, I decided to use the original Spanish term, which many English speakers are familiar with, as it indicates this specific form of narrative writing. I made this choice instead of using the Portuguese translation of the term "Testemunhos." The goal of this choice is to point to the multilingual conversations and exchanges of ideas that are happening across the hemisphere, of which Améfrica Press is an active participant.

# 1

# BLACK TRAVESTIS:
## MIDWIVES OF THE LGBT MOVEMENT

Jovanna Cardoso da Silva[9]
Letícia Carolina Nascimento[10]
Translated by Feibriss Ametista Henrique Meneghelli
Cassilhas and Kukua Dada

The English writer and journalist George Orwell (1903-1950) emphasizes that "history is told by the victors," whether in Brazil, Europe, or the United States, it is always the version told by white, cisheteronormative, Christian, bourgeois, urban men without disabilities. These are not necessarily the winners. Regardless of whether those on the margins win some battles, the version of the socially hegemonic group will prevail.

---

[9] Jovanna Cardoso da Silva is a Black travesti woman, founder of the Brazilian Travestis National Movement, and President of the National Forum of Travestis and Transexuals (FONATRANS).

[10] Leticia Carolina Nascimento is a fat, travesti Black woman, Northeasterner, and of Axé (practitioner of an African-derived religion in Brazil). She is a pedagogue and Professor at the Federal University of Piauí (UFPI) as well as a PhD student in Education (UFPI). She is author of the book Transfeminismo, part of the Feminismos Plurais Collection coordinated by Djamila Ribeiro. She is a researcher linked to ABPN and AINPGP, as well as NEPEGECI/UFPI, RIMAS/UFRPE, and POCs/UFPEL. Nascimento is a social activist working as co-founder and coordinator of the project Acolhe Trans, and she works alongside the national executive coordinators of FONATRANS.

This text invites us to look back at the history of the LGBT movement, recognizing the protagonism of travestis,[11] especially Black travestis. Denouncing the erasure and invisibility that permeates the bodies of Black travestis since the Colony, both in the USA and in Brazil, have challenged cisheteronormative standards and been at the forefront of resistance.

## Between Stones and Erasures: Travestis at Stonewall

Stonewall Inn is the name of a bar in the Greenwich Village neighborhood of New York, frequented by lesbians, travestis, drag queens, and gays. In the early 1960s, the USA was in the process of decriminalizing "homosexual relations." Even though there were no laws prohibiting their gathering at bars, the policing practices, control, and punishments perpetrated by the police, a strong necropolitical arm of the State, were a reality. Although the owners of The Stonewall Inn would bribe the police, the routine police raids did not stop.

In the early morning of June 28, 1969, the LGBT community, tired of the excessive violence that was commonly perpetrated, answered the police operation with protest chants and stone-throwing. On the front lines were a Black travesti named Marsha P. Johnson and a Latina travesti named Sylvia Rivera. Among the many versions of the story, Marsha and Sylvia were the first to throw stones. But the version that popularized the "Stonewall Rebellion" as the beginning of the "gay movement" clearly demonstrates the erasure of travestis' existence.

---

[11] [T.N.] In this article, the authors explain why they use the word travesti to refer to trans people in the USA in the subheading "Marsha and Sylvia: pioneering travestis."

Universalization is dangerous because it leads to erasure within the community. Language is a component that builds our relationships. That which is not named is belittled, devalued, forgotten, and erased. Naming is a political act that shows recognition. By naming a diverse movement that includes a diversity of sexual and gender identities as the "homosexual movement," or the "gay movement," a political exclusion is being carried out. This synthetic form of naming was not a naïve or an unintentional act.

In the years following 1969, the "homosexual movement" elected, as the political subject of its demands, a cis-centered gay white male. Describing this subject's identity with these characteristics is of utmost importance. We shall not underestimate the power of language. Certainly, regarding the characterization of this political subject of the "homosexual movement," we could use only the term "gay," disregarding the term "male." However, such a subject will overvalue a rigidly masculine gender performance to the detriment of "feminine behaviors," which would be marginalized within the community.

Characterizing people as cisgender is also relevant because the masculine gender performances of those gay men are somehow in harmony with what is assumed as their biological sex. Homosexual masculinity reproduces cisheteronormativity. It is important to point out that heterosexuality is not merely a sexual orientation; it creates a political regime, as indicated by the lesbian feminist Monique Wittig (1980).

Also, I understand that cisgendernormativity from the perspective of the Brazilian transfeminist Viviane Vergueiro Simakawa (2015) is not an attribute of heterosexuality. It is a prior critique of the way in which certain identities see themselves as natural, like a harmonic development that emanates from their sexual organs, in a reciprocal relationship between "sex" and "gender." So, it is not incoherent to criticize the way in which the "homosexual movement" articulates itself, after 1969, as being cisheteronormative.

Besides this, the experience of the political subject of the "homosexual movement" assumes a racist archetype. Specifically, it is very important to reinforce that Marsha was Black and that Sylvia was Latina. The idea of white racial supremacy, thoroughly conveyed in the USA, is constructed from not only the political subordination of Black men and women, but also the subordination of the Latin American community. Therefore, the erasure of Marsha and Sylvia serves doubly racist interests.

It is understood that the past and present negotiations of the "homosexual movement" with white/cis/hetero/normativity are a structural consequence of these oppressions. The world is organized based on the interests of white cisheterosexual bodies, and it seems that this is the only way to live our sexuality. This assumption has led some of the homosexuals to confine their desires within norms such as monogamy, marriage, toxic masculinity, and the validation of white aesthetics.

We believe that a revolutionary LGBT movement would be more focused on creating other methods of existing in the world, rather than establishing dangerous relationships with white/cis/hetero/normativity. But this is a discussion for another time. What the LGBT movement needs is the recognition of the historical erasure of travesti identities, in order to regain the transgressive potential of bodies that transgress gender and sexuality norms.

## Marsha and Sylvia: Pioneering Travestis

The LGBTI+ movement needs to understand that Marsha and Sylvia are travestis. That's not a historical incongruity. It is political recognition. The term "travesti" is considered a Latin American category, so it should not be translated into other languages. Therefore, the loose translation is a correlation, not a translation in the strict sense of the word.

Marsha and Sylvia left clues to our understanding that the terms "gay" and/or "drag" were faulty in designating their gender performances. Both founded the Street Transvestite Action Revolutionaries (S.T.A.R.) – the term "transvestite," can be loosely translated as "travesti," because both terms have similar historical roots.

At first, "travestismo" (the word for "transvestism" in Portuguese) was popularly understood as the practice, especially of those assigned male at birth, of wearing clothes associated with women. However, "travesti" emerged slowly as a gender identity, disrupting the idea of a mere customization. A travesti is not someone who is representing the "female gender"; it is an identity. Women (cis and trans) are not naturally female, as well as travestis; both construct their femininity, which is permeated by several discourses. Recognizing Marsha and Sylvia as travestis is to understand the historical processes of resistance that made possible the emergence of travesti gender identities.

S.T.A.R. was a home that cared for young LGBT people and that made it possible to glimpse the fact that travestis, since the beginning of the movement, have always occupied themselves with the construction of inclusive policies. When putting themselves on the front lines, Marsha and Sylvia became the true midwives of the LGBT movement. This is our travesti ancestry: to resist, to crash the normativity of public spaces. Travesti bodies publicize their dissidence with revolutionary acts. After all, the streets belong to travestis. Living on the streets and in other public spaces with our dissident performances is to learn how to live dangerously.

## Brazilian Afro+Trans+Ancestry

Brazilian Afro+Trans+Ancestry emerges from the streets. It is in public spaces that the travesti transforms her corporeity, clothes, and movements into tools to contest cisheteronormativity. In the city of Salvador da Bahia, where the Bay of All Saints is located, Xica Manicongo would walk down the streets like they were her runway, having the audacity to dress in the clothes she considered adequate for her gender performance.

According to transfeminist Professor Jaqueline Gomes de Jesus (2019), Xica Manicongo is the name that the Travesti movement uses to celebrate the ancestral existence of an African female-presenting person from Congo, who was enslaved, sold to a shoemaker, and baptized as Francisco. This was how she was identified until being discovered by her peers. Her existence emerges from historical records based on visits that the Holy Office made to Salvador, Brazil, in 1591.

On that occasion, Xica Manicongo was accused of sodomy. She did not wear "men's clothes," as expected by the cisheteronormative imposition. She used to walk covered with a piece of fabric tied in the front part of her body, just like the quimbandas,[12] indicating that she served as a "patient

---

[12] [E.N.] Quimbandas are practitioners of a religious tradition associated with the West African Orisha Exú and Pombejra (feminine representation of Exú in the Americas). They work with the dead. Quimbanda is commonly understood as Black magic, evil witchcraft, or Satanism. This is largely due to Exú being translated as "Satan" or "Demon" by Christian missionaries, and these deities have been treated as such in the Eurocentric West. Also, Exú, in a precolonial West African context, was understood to be both male and female. Statues and other representations of Exú often show a figure with large breasts and a large erect penis. Exú represents the crossroads, the messenger and mediator between the Orisha and human beings. It is also associated with being a trickster, and as a representation of indeterminacy or unintelligibility. The question of "is it male or is it female?" can lead to various forms of gender trouble, so to speak, from a Eurocentric perspective. However, one can easily argue that these representations are a result of trying to understand Exú outside of historical and cosmological context. Though Exú is now understood by some to be foundational aspect of West African metaphysics, particularly as it pertains to human *being*, male and female, it is still often represented as evil. This belief is also suitably and explicitly present in some of the African-based religious traditions of the African Diaspora in the Americas that continue aspects of precolonial practices centering Exú. See: SILVA, Vagner Gonçalves da. *Exu: um deus afro-atlântico no Brasil*. São Paulo: Editora da Universidade de São Paulo, 2022; and ALEXANDRE, Claudia. *Exu-Mulher e o matriarcado nagô. Sobre masculinização, demonização e tensões de gênero nas formação dos candomblés* (Eshu-Woman and Nagô Matriarchy. About Masculinization, Demonization, and Gender Tensions in Candomble's Formation). Rio de Janeiro: Fundamentos de Axé, 2023, 462p. ISBN 978-65-87, 708-19-5.

woman," or one who served men "as a woman." That is what the Catholic Church and the criminal code considered sodomy, a mortal sin, a nefarious crime that could condemn someone to the stake.

In order not to be murdered, Xica Manicongo had to stop wearing her Congo-style female clothes, so she began to dress according to the masculine norm of the time. Nowadays, Xica Manicongo is celebrated as the first Brazilian travesti in recorded history. Other travestis, or those with experiences in dialogue with these gender identities, must have existed among Brazilians back then, among Indigenous people and people of African descent. However, the historical records and the absence of research make it impossible for us to know them.

If it is true that we need to recognize the travestis Marsha and Sylvia as protagonists, it is also necessary to scrutinize the history of the Brazilian LGBT movement and our resistance. After all, before the political and institutional organization of the LGBT movement, there were resistance processes that need to be acknowledged and valued. Xica Manicongo is a symbol that demonstrates that Black travestis from this country have always been on the front lines of resistance, and she continues to live in our Brazilian Afro+Trans+Ancestry.

## The Organized Social Movement of Travestis and Transsexuals is Born in Brazil

The same process experienced by the LGBT movement in the USA can be observed in Brazil. A group called Somos (meaning "we are" in Portuguese), founded in 1978, the first national organization of this nature, adopted an exclusionary stance, and did not allow the participation of effeminate gays and travestis. It is important to remember that, during the military dictatorship, travestis and effeminate gays were targets of specific police operations, such as Operação Tarântula. Nevertheless, the activism will address the demands from the individual of the LGBT movement "par excellence": the cis-centered white gay man.

The Black travesti Jovanna Cardoso da Silva (2018) tells us that travestis nurtured a severe discontent with the Brazilian Homosexual Movement. Life taught this travesti from the Northeast of Brazil[13] that resistance was not an option; it was a survival strategy. Expelled from home at the age of 13, Jovanna left for Vitória, the capital of Espírito Santo, and the streets became her workplace. In 1979, still in Vitória, this Black travesti participated in the founding of the group Damas da Noite (Ladies of the Night), an organization of cisgender and travesti prostitutes created to denounce police brutality and demand rights.

In the 1980s, Jovanna moved to Rio de Janeiro and, once again, experienced police repression. The background that this northeastern travesti had, in terms of social activism in Vitória, was fundamental to founding ASTRAL (Travestis and Liberados[14] Association), the world's first travesti organization, in 1992, alongside Beatriz Senegal, Elza Lobão, Josy Silva, Monique Du Bavieur, and Claudia Pierry France. These six warriors need to be recognized by the Brazilian LGBTI+ movement. They are the founders of the worldwide organized social and political travesti and transgender movement. Moreover, Jovanna Cardoso, Beatriz Senegal, and Josy Silva are still alive and need to be celebrated! Josy Silva is alive, but we don't have her contact information.

---

[13] [E.N.] Culturally, the Northeast of Brazil is seen vary much through a similar lens of the U S. Southeast. It is seen as largely Black, underdeveloped, backwards. It is a racialized, stigmatized and marginalized region, as it is seen as the region with the most intense African Influence, and cultural retention, in comparison to the rest of the country.

[14] [T.N.] According to Jovanna Baby, Liberados were gay men who dressed as women to work as prostitutes. They resorted to this measure to ensure their survival, and ASTRAL recognized the importance of including them in their initiatives. Source: https://www.facebook.com/reel/879890349135062. Accessed on July 16, 2025.

When it comes to Jovanna, she is currently the *PresidentTRA*[15] of the National Forum of Black Travestis and Transsexuals (FONATRANS). Since the 1990s, she has been considered one of the main leaders of the Brazilian trans movement. Beatriz Senegal currently lives in Barcelona, Spain. She has been on the cover of magazines, calendars, and reports, with big titles such as "O Reino das Cafetinas" (Kingdom of Madams) and "Camaleoa Invencível" (Invincible Chameleon). This highlights the strength of the carioca's[16] resistance. The co-founder of the travesti movement in Brazil continues to represent ASTRAL in political activities in Europe. Her activism includes fighting against the international trafficking of women and travestis for prostitution. If the USA has Marsha and Sylvia, we have Jovanna and Beatriz, as well as Elza Lobão, Josy Silva, Monique Du Bavieur, Claudia Pierry France, and many others.

## Our Silence Will Not Protect Us: Black Travestis Telling Their Stories

The Black Latina-Caribbean feminist Audre Lorde teaches us that our silence will not protect us. Hence, it is necessary to raise our voices and disrupt the invisibility of our stories. Our trajectory of resistance needs to be known within the LGBT movement, because Black travestis have a trajectory of resistance. It is important to learn from our differences. Even though white *ciscentered* gay men experience violence, they have different access compared to us, travestis, so they can play an important role in disrupting the segregation imposed on them at one time.

---

[15] In Portuguese we have the word *presidente*, which can be used for both men and women, but we also have the word *presidenta*, used only to refer to women. Dilma Rousseff, the first female elected president of Brazil, preferred being called *presidenta* instead of *presidente*. *PresidenTRA* is a neologism combining the word *presidenta* with the first syllable of the word *travesti*.

[16] [E.N.] Carioca is a term that refers to people from Rio de Janeiro. Here the author is referring to Beatriz Senegal as a person from Rio de Janeiro.

We, Black travestis, want to be reckoned with and celebrated as protagonists. If we put ourselves on the front line of resistance, it is because our lives are already on the front line; we are the ones with the highest number of deaths. Data from ANTRA and IBTE (BENEVIDES; NOGUEIRA, 2021) reveals that 78% of the lethal victims of transphobia in 2020 were Black or Parda.[17]

That is why it is so important to celebrate not only our stories, but also our hopes, and, as a consequence, the wish to be alive and fighting for our lives. Listening to and telling our stories allows us to dream. When I listen to the voices of Jovanna and Beatriz, my personal friends, my heart is filled with hope and strength. We need to cherish the roots to the blossom. We need to repeat their names and tell their stories so that they do not sink into oblivion.

We, Black travestis who started occupying places that were unthinkable for us, are daughters of Xica Manicongo's ancestry; heirs to the strength of Marsha P. Johnson and Sylvia Rivera; and successors to the dreams of Jovanna Cardoso, Beatriz Senegal, Elza Lobão, Josy Silva, Monique Du Bavieur, and Claudia Pierry France. To live is to resist, and also a way of celebrating the memories of our Black travesti sisters. The door was opened by them; we need to keep paving the way, keep moving forward. Xica Manicongo lives![18]

---

[17] [E.N.] In Brazil, *parda/o* refers to a person who appears to be mixed race. It is a category used in the official census to classify individuals with ancestry from multiple racial backgrounds, including Indigenous, African, and European origins. Who gets classified as such is subjective and varies across the region, both for the person themselves and the person who is determining their race. Regional variations for racial categories are common throughout the West. [T.N.] According to the Brazilian Institute of Geography and Statistics (IBGE), Pardo refers to individuals who self-identify as Pardo and are mixed race, with a predominance of Black traits.

[18] This article was originally published July 16, 2020 on the Nohs Somos blog. Its publication in this collection was authorized by the author Leticia Nascimento dos Santos. The text was reviewed by Jovanna Cardoso. You can access the original post, written in Portuguese, at:

## REFERENCES

BENEVIDES, Bruna G.; NOGUEIRA, Sayonara Naider Bonfim (orgs). **Dossiê dos assassinatos e da violência contra travestis e transexuais brasileiras em 2020**. São Paulo: Expressão Popular, Antra, IBTE, 2021.

JESUS, Jaqueline Gomes de. **Xica Manicongo: a transgeneridade toma a palavra**. Revista Docência e Cibercultura. Rio de Janeiro, v. 3, n. 1, jan-abr. 2019.

SILVA, Jovanna Cardoso da. Movimento político social da população T no Brasil. In: CAETANO, Márcio [et al] (orgs.). **Quando ousamos existir: itinerários fotobiográficos do movimento LGBTI Brasileiro (1978-2018)**. Tubarão: Copiart; Rio Grande, RS: FURG, 2018.

SIMAKAWA, Viviane Vergueiro. **Por inflexões decoloniais de corpos e identidades de gênero in conformes: uma análise autoetnográfica da cisgeneridade como normatividade**. Thesis (Multidisciplinary Master's Program in Culture and Society)—Instituto de Humanidades, Artes e Ciências Professor Milton Santos. Salvador: Universidade Federal da Bahia, 2015, 244 f.

WITTIG, Monique. **O pensamento hétero**. EUA: 1980. Available at: https://pt.scribd.com/document/266100494/Wittig-Monique--O-Pensamento-Hetero-pdf. Last accessed July 20, 2021.

---

https://nohssomos.com.br/2020/07/18/travestis-negras-parteiras-do-movimento-lgbt/. Accessed July 20, 2021. [E.N.] As of Monday, September 1, 2025, The link appears in a google search, but opening the actual website does not work.

# 2

# WHO CARES ABOUT THE SOLIDÃO OF BLACK TRANSGENDER WOMEN FROM THE PERIPHERY?

Ariane Moreira de Senna[19]
Translated by Feibriss Ametista Henrique Meneghelli Cassilhas, and Kukua Dada

Once I was at a movie debate where the film "Get Out" (2017) was exhibited. The main plot revolves around a white, middle-class Woman who lures and captures Black men and Women, while deluding them into believing they are her possible boyfriends or girlfriends, in order to put them through a violent procedure that can be compared to slavery. After the movie screening, when the debate started, I shared my perspective about it. Among them, for instance, the fact that there was no coincidence that the director had chosen a white Woman to allure and capture Black males. This

---

[19] Ariane Moreira de Senna is a psychologist and Masters student in Ethnic and African Studies at the Center for Afro-Oriental Studies (CEAO) at the Federal University of Bahia, where she researches the Solidão of Black trans women from the periphery. [E.N.] RAMOS SILVA, Luciane; SAUNDERS, Tanya L.; OHMER, Sarah Soanirina (eds.). *Women's Studies Quarterly. Special Issue on Solidão/Black Women's Affect*. Women's Studies Quarterly, New York, v. 49, n. 1, 2021.

demonstrates the constant "palmitagem,"[20] in which Black men are seduced by white Women, contributing to what the teacher Ana Cláudia Pacheco (2013) calls the Black Women's *solidão*.

At that moment, a white professor, who organized the venue for the activity, reacted immediately to my remarks. She affirmed that she was a Woman who raised her kids by herself and that I could not use the term Black Women *solidão* because that would be generalizing. She kept arguing that we should be more supportive of each other, implying that the term "palmitagem" connotes self-interest.

Given her confrontational speech, I answered that I had no doubt whatsoever that what she had brought attention to was a reality (the *solidão* of the white Women). However, I argued, such *solidão* is disproportionate to the *solidão* that was and is experienced by Black Women. My argument continued, highlighting that it was impossible to compare both realities because racism is embedded in Brazil's institutions. Moreover, stereotypes surrounding Black Women persist. They are regarded as filthy, the house slave, objectified, hired for physically demanding work only, and regarded as promiscuous, besides the many other names from the colonial period's slavery.

She rejected my argument and kept hitting back, arguing that she was lonely, even though she was a middle-class white Woman. Given her tenacity, I clarified my thoughts and told her that I had not meant to diminish her reality, one that is specific and from an individual perspective; however, Black Women's realities are structural and of a collective

---

[20] [T.N.] Palmitagem is a word in Brazilian Portuguese to originally describe the social phenomenon of the cisgender heterosexual Black men who prioritizes dating white women. Palmitagem comes from the word *palmito*, which is the Portuguese word for "palm heart" and a reference to the white skin color. This word became very popular and can be used to describe any Black person with the same behavior, regardless of gender and sexuality, however, some people still stick to the traditional definition.

perspective. *Solidão*, for some Black Women, can also be seen from a personal viewpoint. If we take into consideration one's skin tone (e.g. the lighter the skin, the more attractive), and their socioeconomic status (higher socioeconomic status correlates with increased opportunities, which does not necessarily imply acceptance, but they would be able to share exclusive environments with high-society individuals and find a romantic and sexual partner).

I explained to her that, in fact, cis white and cis Black Women may experience social isolation because of the constructions and roles assigned to Women in society. Consequently, cis Women were placed in a submissive position by men nonstop. But, while white Women are likely to be seen as fluffy and domesticated poodle puppies by men (those that are cared for at home, and get to walk on the streets with their keepers), the Black Women would be the stray dogs, those on the street that you may touch or pet, but who must remain on the streets because they are too ugly to be adopted.

She did not understand yet, so I did not even try to bring up the discussion about trans Black Women's *solidão* because, undoubtedly, it would become an endless argument. For a long time, the debate was on this issue of *solidão*, just one of the points I raised in that space. In this sense, Professor Ana Cláudia Pacheco (2013) brings up the following reflection in her work: "Why is it so uncomfortable to talk about the *solidão* of Black Women?" To this, I add another question: Why is it that I am so often placed in a position of victimization and of less importance when I speak, write, and denounce the *solidão* of Black and peripheral trans Women? I had to cultivate profound self-confidence and persist so that this theme would be accepted as my master's thesis project. My objective is that you'll get the importance of addressing this issue while reading this text.

The *solidão* of the Black Trans Women from the periphery goes far beyond the idea of conjugal relationships, of simply debating the presence or absence of romantic and sexual partnership dynamics. It characterizes our whole lives since childhood, or at least since initiating our gender transitions, when most of us begin to endure perverse forms of surveillance in our homes (when we do not experience displacement, as it happened to me). Our relationship with *solidão* and beauty converges when we start investing in body modifications and in maintaining the symbols of good appearance and femininity, while believing that this would increase our social acceptance. And it also affects the relationship between *solidão* and acceptance, or not, of our own bodies (the famous gender dysphoria), culminating in the relationship between *solidão* and prostitution (when we fail to discover alternative means of survival), among other relations that I point out in my dissertation.

When I have it in mind to think about the structural *solidão* that permeates the gender marker of being a Woman, it is to understand that we live within a structure that has historically placed us in a non-place. This results in the lack of rights and the lack of recognition of our citizenship. This process has been experienced for a long time, as it still is, even by cisgender Women, simply because they are Women. Considering that they have to fight for their rights to live in a society where the rights of men are already established as something static and natural.

Likewise, when I point out that it is a loneliness also marked by the dimension of race, it is because I understand the struggle that we Black Women have been fighting to be recognized as people. The inferior places in work, employment, and income are historical, and this is also marked by the way we dress, the quality of the clothes, fabrics, jewelry, and shoes that they permit us to wear, according to our capacity to enjoy something. I remember, for example, that in one of the activities that I organize at the Public Defender's Office of the State of Bahia (where I currently work), the guest, professor of the bachelor's degree in Gender and Diversity Studies at the Federal University of Bahia, Carol Barreto, said that "we wear race." In other words, she pointed out that others recognize us as belonging to a certain race only by the way we present ourselves socially.

Taking into account the historical connection between race and class in a place of subalternity, Kimberlé Crenshaw (2004) coined the term "intersectionality," especially to say that a Black Woman's body never reflects just one axis of oppression, but two or more that are added to the social markers that we carry in our bodies. Therefore, I am talking about the *solidão* of erasure that harries our existences and our subjectivities. It is the true social death that kills us way before physical death.

Beyond the dimensions of gender and race, I have been thinking a lot about the marker of being someone who is trans and from the periphery, and about the history of the bodies that occupy the periphery. The downer category, for example, is closely related to travestis and trans Women who are black and from the periphery. A scenario that changes when it comes to a middle-class trans white Woman, who experienced several years of prostitution, including in Europe, who prepared themselves financially in order to save money and return to Brazil, with belongings that enable a place of "independence" in society. The idea of downer-ness is distant from travestis and trans Women who achieved status and/or a good level of education, since socially they are seen as different, as "easygoing" and as people who know how to behave.

The travestis and transsexuals classified as downers also refer to those who are loud, who yell, who "sexualize", and who society identifies as *traveção*[21]. In my perspective, these are all behaviors, attitudes, and clothing that are used as defense and adaptation, so that we can deal in the best way we can with the cis-tem to which we are subjected: the periphery. Thus, "speaking too loud" or shouting, which we often do, may just be a way of

---

[21] [T.N] A word, often used with a negative connotation, to describe travestis and trans Women associating them with the masculine gender.

believing that, by doing that, we could make people respect us, to see us so that they do not kill us.

In this context, we also need to reflect on the reasons why many of us walk "half-naked," for example. While this behavior can be understood as vulgar by some people, on the contrary, it can just be a way for us to expose parts of our bodies in order to remind our neighbors - who have seen us since our birth, who saw us growing up going through a process of wearing male clothes and who are also aware that we are trans—that our bodies now have breasts and curves (symbols of femininity). It becomes a way to present the great Women we have become. It's a way of asking, indirectly, through our bodies, "Can't you see this Woman's body?"

The lack of understanding of our subjectivities has placed us in a much more profound place of *solidão*, of social *solidão*. After all, who wants to be embarrassed? Who enjoys vulgarity? Who would invite this type of person to join their friends and family for coffee or dinner? Before bringing up the fact that Brazil is the country with the highest number of travestis and transgender people murdered per year in the world, we need to talk about this social death, which turns us invisible all the time—even when so many of us ask for help through posts on social media, reporting our dismay and the sadness of living a lonely life. Who cares about the *solidão* of the Black transgender Women from the periphery?

We, Black trans Women from the periphery, are submitted to conditions that impel us to feel down and lonely—conditions established by society as a whole, a *solidão* that is legitimized mostly by the state, when it does not make a single move to provide humanizing conditions such as housing, education, health care, employment opportunities, income, leisure and safety for our population.

The *solidão* of Black trans Women from the periphery, most of the time, begins with family rejection, but it only ends in death, when we are brutally murdered, often by the same people we share a relationship with, which can be social-affective and/or sexual partners, such as settled partners, prostitution clients, or even friends. The existences and relationships that we build are the same ones that extinguish us. Therefore, I am talking about the *solidão* of not being recognized as citizens.

Years come and go, and we still struggle to be called by our preferred names. We fight so that they let us live in peace, so that they stop forcing us into prostitution, to live in marginalized spaces, where we normally don't even receive a visit from the public authorities to check the subhuman conditions in which we live. I'm talking about precarious boarding houses and occupations that heighten vulnerability. But, unfortunately, we lack access to better alternatives. Who cares about the *solidão* of the Black transgender Women from the periphery?

## REFERENCES

PEELE, Jordan. **Get Out!** USA: Universal, 2017. 1 DVD, 1h44m.

CRENSHAW, Kimberly. **A interseccionalidade na discriminação entre raça e gênero.** In: VV.AA. **Cruzamento: raça e gênero**. Brasília, Unifem, 2004, p. 7-16.

PACHECO, Ana Cláudia Lemos. **Mulher negra: afetividade e solidão.** Coleção Temas Afro Salvador. EDUFBA, 2013, p. 382.

# 3

# TURNING HOLY INTO DANGEROUS:
## TRANSFEMININE BODIES, REPRESENTATION, AND ERASURES IN THE VISUAL ARTS BY THE 19TH CENTURY

Megg Rayara Gomes de Oliveira[22]
Translated by Ale Mujica, Feibriss Ametista Henrique
Meneghelli Cassilhas, and Ti Ochoa

## Introduction

Since the body is the material substance, the figure could be explained as its external form, its image, and its representation.

The physical body is tangible, in contrast to the image, which resides in the domain of symbols and representation. Therefore, the built image also carries political implications. Each epoch has its own visual representations that mirror the prevailing social codes. By accessing these codes and representational socio-cultural norms, we recognize, identify, name, and produce them, thereby providing meaning grounded in context.

---

[22] Megg Rayara Gomes de Oliveira is a Black travesti, with a Doctorate, and Masters in Education from the Federal University of Paraná. Dr. Gomes de Oliveria is a research specialist in African and Afro-Brazilian History and Culture, Education, and Affirmative Action in Brazil from Tuiuti University of Paraná, Specialist in Art History, she graduated with a degree in Drawing from the School of Music and Fine Arts of Paraná. She is currently the coordinator of the NEAB—Center for Afro-Brazilian Studies at the Federal University of Paraná.

The meaning attributed to an image may diverge from its creator's expectations, as it is subject to various mediations, many of which are influenced by preconceived notions, biases, and stereotypes.

Despite the absence of a "coherent system for reading images akin to that created for reading writing" (Alberto MANGUEL, 2001, p. 28, our translation),[23] it is possible to consider that a universalizing visual language has emerged in contemporary societies. Despite cultural differences and the specificity of many aesthetic codes.

Universalization is evident in elements that facilitate image comprehension, even among those without formal visual literacy, "for what is presented to the reader through writing, paintings—*that is, images*—presents for the illiterate" (MANGUEL, 2001, p. 143, our translation, emphasis added).

I argue that even prior to the advent of writing, images already played a crucial role in disseminating certain ways of thinking, serving as a tool to affirm or question power dynamics. Throughout the vast expanse of art history—African, European, American, and beyond—the most common image has been that of the human figure. The most disseminated representations here in Brazil are those from Western art, in which the young, slim, cisgender, heterosexual white man is portrayed as the "self;" in other words, the "universal model of the human being" (Paulo Vinícius Baptista da SILVA, 2008, our translation).

Thus, bodies that deviate from this standard of beauty are considered inadequate by the reasoning of the white heterosexual cisgender norms imposed by the European standard of civilization, deserve to be, and should be, ignored. If represented, they are often depicted in ways that reaffirm their presumed inferiority.

---

[23] In support of gender-inclusive education, I use both feminine and masculine genders when referring to individuals. Upon first citation, authors' full names are provided to acknowledge gender and increase visibility for female researchers and scholars.

Amid the multitude of bodies systematically erased from the visual arts, this article sheds light on the discussion surrounding Black and white trans feminine bodies — specifically travestis and/or transgender women. Despite their scarcity in the history of visual arts as a theme, I believe it is important to question the circumstances under which this erasure occurs and to highlight the elements that contribute to travesti and transender women's representation and/or exclusion.

This study endeavors to contribute, with modest ambitions, to disrupting the relative invisibility surrounding the representation of white and Black travestis and/or transgender women in the visual arts. I aim to identify works and artists who have portrayed them across various time periods and cultures up to the 19th century.

For the purposes of this analysis, I will take into consideration two-dimensional works—drawing, painting, engraving, illustration, photography, bas-relief, watercolor, etc.—as well as three-dimensional works, particularly sculptures.

Building on Inês Dussel and Marcelo Caruso's (2003) genealogical framework, this research undertakes a critical and engaged approach to both Universal History and Art History, as well as highlights how art history intersects significantly with Donna Haraway's (1995) concept of Universal History.

According to Haraway, History can be defined as a technology of the gaze. A scrutinized gaze at the perfection of capitalism, colonialism, and male supremacy; a situated knowledge arising from the bodies that matter and, therefore, deserve to be remembered (HARAWAY, 1995).

Through directing a particular gaze, one that questions the invisibility of transgender women and/or travestis in the History of Art, this genealogy enables a nuanced analysis of this situation. I understand that this genealogy needs to be integrated with other fields of knowledge; therefore, I point to the concept of intersectionality developed by American lawyer Kimberlé

Crenshaw in 1989 (Mara Viveros VIGOYA, 2016), as it enables the analysis of class, gender, gender identity, and race issues simultaneously.

Through a genealogical approach, the concept of intersectionality, combined with the cultural and post-structuralist perspective, feminist studies, ethnic and racial studies, and gender studies, offers the theoretical and methodological foundations to locate, identify, and highlight works and artists that feature the bodies of transgender women and travestis in the visual arts up to the 19th century.

## Astonishing, sacred, and powerful!

Throughout human history, there have been countless examples of images depicting transfeminine bodies. However, tracing a chronological line of these works becomes quite complicated, given the numerous observable gaps in both Universal History and Art History. I understand that these gaps have not been adequately filled deliberately, as they are associated with hierarchies of race and gender and serve to convey the idea of the non-existence of travestis and/or transgender women.

Few studies address this subject in the visual arts; even the most recent ones adopt multiple terminologies, such as "hermaphrodite"[24] and/or "androgynous." Others still do not make "the distinction between sexual orientation and gender identity" (Fernanda Dantas VIEIRA, 2015, n.p., our translation), and treat travestis and transgender women as a specific category of male homosexuals. Thus, the definition of the concepts of androgynous and/or hermaphrodite "aim to describe people who exhibited bodily features in which attributes culturally constructed as masculine and feminine were integrated" (Megg Rayara Gomes de OLIVEIRA, 2019, n.p., our translation).

---

[24] The term "hermaphrodite" has been replaced by "intersex" in both medical and social contexts.

Hence, I assert that these concepts relate to individuals who defy the normativity of cisgender identity and, consequently, "the traditional existing polarities between masculinity and femininity, as well as the essentialist perspective that "biologically determines" gender, prioritizing two distinct, consistent, and fixed biological sexes" (Jean Carlo Silva dos SANTOS, 2013, p. 95, our translation).

"Based on these reflections, and for the purposes of this article, I took the liberty to employ the terms "travesti," "transgender women," and/or "trans people" instead of "androgynous" and "hermaphrodite," revisiting and redefining both concepts" (OLIVEIRA, 2018, p. 79, our translation), except in direct or indirect quotation contexts.

This research has led me down multiple paths, and I identify the earliest representations of transfeminine bodies within sacred contexts dating back to the Neolithic Period (5,000 to 3,000 B.C.) and the Bronze Age (3,300 to 700 B.C.). Drawings and paintings from these periods were identified in the Mediterranean region, featuring human figures with female breasts and male genitalia, or not having a sexual characteristic that distinguished them.

These representations, like the majority of cave paintings, were more than just decorations; evidence suggests that they "have a religious value, with symbols linked to magic" (Rodrigo Simas AGUIAR, 2012, our translation). It is also possible to assume that such images likely originated from everyday experiences, deriving from observations of the real world. The attributed meaning, then, would be inextricably linked to religious purposes.

Some researchers (Pierre VERGER, 1999; Raymundo Nina RODRIGUES, 2010; Peter JONES, 2006) have indicated that both religious and artistic practices reflect the social dynamics of a people to a varying extent. Thus, the multiplicity of genres present in religion and in art is constantly identified among individuals, suggesting that the worship of deities that transcend the norms of cisgender identity is not part of a less meaningful chapter in the history of religions and humanity.

The American Catholic theologian Peter Jones (2006) listed a series of deities that share similarities with contemporary travestis and/or transgender women, having breasts and penises, and who are also named and referred to in feminine terms. He also documented rituals where religious leaders, biologically male, adopt gestures and clothing considered typical of the female universe (OLIVEIRA, 2019, n.p.). Among the deities mentioned by Jones (2006), some became very popular, such as Ardhanarishvara, a fusion of Shiva and his wife Parvati, who represents the union of the two genders and symbolizes, for Hindus in India, the beginning of everything.

This deity has been extensively depicted in drawings, paintings, tapestries, and especially sculptures displayed in temples and public spaces. For Hindus, art "is an encounter of two poles, the human and the divine. Therefore, the sculptural representations of the gods had theological and narrative purposes" (Joachim ANDRADE, 2006, p. 7, our translation). Art, in addition to pleasing the eye, was inevitably meant to please the spirit.

In Indian culture, transgender women held sacred status approximately 5,000 years ago. Known as Hijras, they enjoyed considerable tranquility in expressing their identity freely before contact with European culture, which was heavily influenced by christianism. Ana Lúcia Fonseca Santos (2012) notes that Hijra identity has a mythical origin and is believed to possess the powers of blessing and cursing, which is why they are respected and/or feared by the population.

**FIGURE 1**
Ardhanarishvara, 6th Century
Government Museum, Rajasthan, India
**Source: Encyclopedia Britannica**[25]

---

[25] Image available at: https://www.britannica.com/topic/Ardhanarishvara. Accessed Monday, September 1, 2025 at 10:20 pm.

In Tibet, Jones (2006) cataloged the hidden Avalokiteshvara[26], a deity characterized by gender fluidity, and represented in sculptures and paintings in male form, with mustaches and weapons, and in the form of a beautiful woman wearing a dress. Just as in Asia, transgender deities have also influenced many African artists, both in traditional art[27] and in Egyptian art.

According to Pierre Verger (1999) and Raymundo Nina Rodrigues (2010), the list of African transgender deities[28] is quite substantial, including Obatalá, Mawu-Lisa, and Nana Buluku in the kingdom of Dahomey, Mwari among the Shona people, Aku and Awo in the Akan kingdom, and Hapi, the god/goddess of the Nile River in ancient Egypt. Hapi is likely one of the oldest deities worshiped by the Egyptians, given its association with the Nile River. Depicted with breasts, rounded hips, and a beard, Hapi symbolizes the fertility brought by the annual flooding.

Egyptian art is also the one that documents one of the earliest historical figures, the "deliberately androgynous Akhenaten (Amenhotep IV), Pharaoh of the 18th Dynasty,[29] whose reign was characterized by profound transformations in political, religious, and artistic fields" (Maria BERBARA; Raphael FONSECA, 2011, p. 2239, our translation).

Akhenaten's bodily representations[30], characterized by feminine features (elongated face, bust, wide hips, protruding abdomen), correlate with the archetype of the god Aton, identified with the solar disk and regarded as the father and mother of all things (BERBARA; FONSECA, 2011).

---

[26] [E.N.] Shown in Figure 1.

[27] Traditional art refers to traditional peoples, culturally distinct groups who have their own social structures rooted in precolonial cultures.

[28] Verger (1999) and Rodrigues (2010) use the term androgynous to refer to these deities.

[29] The Eighteenth Dynasty spanned the period from 1550/1549 BC to 1292 BC.

[30] [E.N.] Shown in Figure 2.

**FIGURE 2**
Hapi, bas-relief, temple of the goddess Hathor
Dendera Complex, Egypt
**Source: Page dedicated to Ancient Egypt**[31]

---

[31] Image available at: https://antigoegito.org/rio-nilo-uma-dadiva/. Accessed July 20, 2021.

Portrayed with both masculine and feminine characteristics, Akhenaten assumed the form of an absolute supreme being, similar to other African cultures.

The Dogon people, who are currently situated in Mali, for instance, believed that a body with characteristics of both sexes and genders represents the perfect body (OLIVEIRA, 2018). The Dogon arrived in the Bandiagara region of Mali, a geological fracture located in an area of about 200 km long situated between the savannah and the Niger River plain, in the 15th century. Similar to Indians, Tibetans, and Egyptians, the Dogon worldview was manifested in their artistic production.

The trans[32] figure of the Master of Yayé is currently displayed at the Louvre Museum in Paris, after being brought to France in 1935 by researchers Denise Paulme and Debora Lifchitz (Jair GUILHERME FILHO, 2014)[33]. It serves as an illustrative case. This wooden sculpture presents a nude figure, with exposed penis and breasts, and illustrates the Dogon's standards of perfection.

Among the various styles of Dogon sculpture that depict transfeminine bodies, the Niongom, Tellem, and Djen-nenké styles stand out. A work in the Tellem style is displayed at the Metropolitan Museum in New York and portrays a tall trans figure "with her hat, her necklace of square plates, her bracelets and armlets, and a belt accentuating the naked sexual anatomy, and both arms raised as if she were a Tellem." (Alberto da Costa e SILVA, 2006, p. 651, our translation).

To understand Dogon art, according to Hélène Leulop (2010), one must acknowledge that the Dogon concept of perfection arises from the reconnection of what has been separated and the transgression of gender binarism, which consequently the ultimate outcome leads to perfection.

---

[32] Jair Guilherme Filho (2012) employs the term "hermaphrodite" in reference to the work.

[33] [E.N.] Shown in Figure 3.

The masks used in the N'domo initiation ceremonies of the Bambara people of Mali can be masculine, feminine, and trans. In this context, the number of horns serves as a gender indicator: seven-horned masks represent gender fluidity. Children who have not been initiated yet or who have transitioned between genders are linked to mythical ancestors, often represented by transgender figures or by a pair consisting of a cisgender male figure and a cisgender female figure (OLIVEIRA, 2019, n.p.).

This diversity of bodies in African religiosity—connected, according to Jones (2006), to sexual freedom and gender diversity among these populations—is also observed, although to a lesser extent, in Greek and Roman cultures. For example, the most popular Greek deity that escapes hegemonic cisgender norms was called Hermaphroditus, the child of Hermes and Aphrodite, and first appears in Greek literature around the 4th century B.C. However, it is Ovid's stories that effectively establish the identity of this myth" (Pérola de Paula SANFELICE, 2013, p. 18, our translation).

According to Aileen Ajootian (2004), Hermaphroditus was represented in four main ways: Hermaphroditus alone, naked or half-naked; Hermaphroditus alone, dressed; Hermaphroditus sleeping; and Hermaphroditus in the presence of others. The fusion of masculine and feminine genders made Hermaphroditus the guardian of human fertility. Breasts were considered symbols of fertility, evoking breastfeeding, and were linked to feminine vital power. Similarly, the penis was associated with fertility, making explicit references to copulation, thus carrying an extremely positive and religious connotation (SANFELICE, 2013).

**FIGURE 3**
Hermaphrodite with the arms raised, Djennenké style, 10th century, Quai Branly Museum, Paris

**Source: Itinerary, Aesthetic and Stylistic Study of a Dogon Sculpture: "Hermaphrodite Figure" by the Master of YaYé[34]**

---

[34] Source: DOCPLAYER-Itinerário, Estudo Estético e Estilístico de uma escultura Dogon: "figura Hermafrodi- ta" do Mestre de YaYé. Image available at: http://docplayer.com.br/45453346-Itinerario-estudo-estetico-e-estilistico-de-uma-escultura-dogon-figura-hermafrodita-do-mestre-de-yaye.html. Accessed on: July 20, 2021. [E.N.] this link is no longer active. We were able to find a photo of the sculpture at the Musée Du Quai

Hence, images of Hermaphroditus have been found in a variety of contexts and environments, in the form of both sculpture and painting. Hermaphroditus was present at the entrances of houses; for example, there were paintings, and a sculpture discovered at the entrance of the House of the Vettii and in the main room of the House of the Centenary (SANFELICE, 2013), in the city of Pompeii, buried by the eruption of Mount Vesuvius in the year 79 AD. The Roman works were likely inspired by Greek originals.

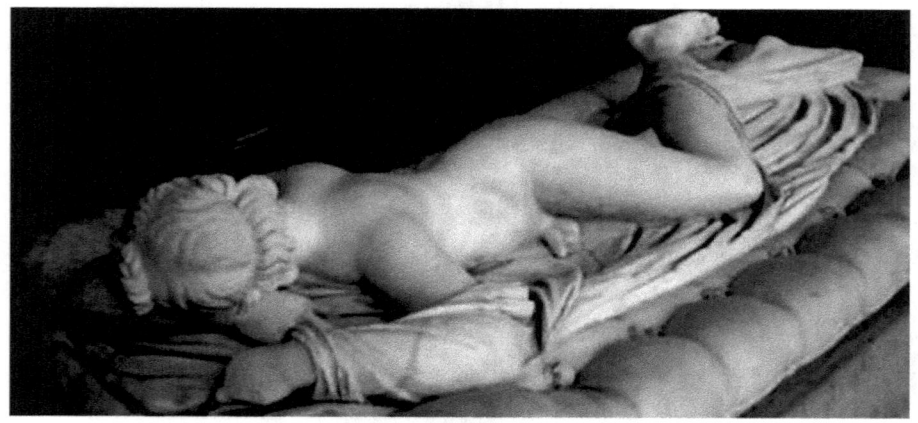

**FIGURE 4**
Sleeping Hermaphroditus, marble, 2nd century A.D.,
Louvre Museum, Paris.
**Source: FLICKR Page[35]**

---

Branly-Jacques Chirac - https://www.quaibranly.fr/en/, where it is currently housed. This photo is listed on the museum's website. The photo can be found through a website search for "Statue anthropomorphe." Last accessed July 14, 2025.

[35] Image available at: https://www.flickr.com/photos/mager-son/5151753750. Accessed July 20, 2021. [E.N.] this link no longer works. However, a copy of the image can be found here: https://en.m.wikipedia.org/wiki/File:Hermafrodita_2.JPG. Last accessed July 14th, 2025.

A Greek bronze sculpture, probably from the 2nd century B.C., was used as a model for some Roman artists. "Three marble copies from the Roman era survived to our time. The most well-known was found in the Baths of Diocletian ruins[36] and is now housed in the Louvre Museum. The body is inspired by representations of Venus (Anchyses Jobim LOPES, 2017, p. 62, our translation), albeit with a penis. Life-sized, the figure delicately reclines on a mattress sculpted by the Italian artist Gian Lorenzo Bernini in 1620. When the sculpture was discovered at Santa Maria della Vittoria in Rome, it was immediately claimed by Cardinal Scipione Borghese, and since then, it has been part of his private collection. The sculpture was later sold to the French army and ultimately ended up in the Louvre Museum, where it is currently housed.

Hermaphroditus has garnered various interpretations and names; nonetheless, its main physical characteristics have been preserved to facilitate identification. A good example is the Statue of Narcissus, known as Marazin Hermaphrodite or The Genius of Eternal Rest, a Roman piece crafted in marble in the 3rd century AD, which is also housed at the Louvre Museum in Paris. It depicts Narcissus with a feminized face and body, featuring developing breasts and a penis. Another sculpture that has survived to this day depicts a struggle between Hermaphroditus and the god Pan. The main figure, although headless, adheres to the same rules of representation, featuring breasts, feminine curves, and gestures, while displaying male genitalia, confirming that it represents a trans body.
As reported in the Christie's auction catalog:

> The ensemble was sculpted during the early period of the Roman Empire, around the 1st century A.D., but is based on an original from the mid-2nd century B.C., when illustrations depicting

---

[36] The Baths of Diocletian were constructed between the years 298 and 306.

confrontations between beastly forces and a Hermaphrodite nymph were immensely popular (WORDPRESS, 2011, n.p., our translation).

## Banished, forgotten, erased: trans female bodies in European art

Although there are countless examples of Greek and Roman works depicting Hermaphroditus, the cisnormativity (the cisgenderedness or cisgender norm) has operated to exclude them from galleries, museums, and especially from the History of Art.

Based on the reflections of Michel Foucault (1926-1984) in the text Herculine Barbin: The Diary of a Hermaphrodite (1982), Sanfelice (2013) explains that the social proposals in practice, at the time of the discovery of these works [and which still have an impact on contemporary societies], were exclusion (banishment, exile, erasure) or prohibition (correction, cure, monstrification). Given that the search for identity, in the [emergent] sexual order, was increasingly practiced by Medicine and Law[37], it imposed a rigid norm in the definition and assessment of the 'true' sex of individuals.

Thus, it was essential that society remain distanced from this model of the body. And it was up to those responsible for the aesthetics of European visual arts in the 19th and 20th centuries, to select what was worthy of admiration and what should remain hidden or locked away in guarded rooms (NEAD, 2001 apud SANFELICE, 2013).

---

[37] Even though medicine and law were established as sciences, Christianity exerted significant influence upon them.

**FIGURE 5**
Author unknown,
Salmacis: neither one nor the other, 1885
**Source: Dexedrina blog page**[38]

These actions, however severe they may have been, were unable to prevent some works considered inappropriate from reaching the exhibition halls of some museums, given the existence of a very extensive list of European artists who, from the 15th century onwards, took an interest in the myth of Hermaphroditus and portrayed it mainly in the form of engravings and paintings.

Among them, it is possible to identify: Maestro Flamenco, Hermaphroditus, and Salmacist, sec. XV; Louis Finson, Hermaphroditus

---

[38] Image available at: http://dexedrina.blogspot.com/2010/05/hermafrodito-y-salmacis.html. Last accessed July 20, 2021.

and Salmacis, oil on canvas, 1580-1585; Jan Gossaert (Mabuse), La metamorfosis de hermafrodito y Salmacis, 1520; Bartholomaus Spranger, Hermaphroditus y la ninfa Salmacis, 1580-82; Carlo Saraceni, Paisage com Salmaci y e Hermafrodito, 1608; Francesco Albani, Salmacis and Hermaphroditus, 1660; Jean François de Troy, Salmacis y Hermafrodito, 1708; François Joseph Navez, The Nymph Salmacis and Hermaphroditus, 1829; Gante Giovanni Carnovali, Salmace e Ermafrodito, oil on canvas, 1856.

These artworks, however, follow more restrained rules of representation, and the myth of Hermaphroditus is rarely shown with the same narrative freedom seen in Greek and Roman art. Still, keeping the proper proportions in mind, they offer another discursive possibility with regard to the body.

This restraint is probably related to the surveillance imposed by christianism, which demanded that the state, even in the European colonies in America and Africa, eliminate trans people, either by forcibly returning them to cisnormativity or by condemning them to death.

The church's actions, explains Jocélio Teles dos Santos (1996), found support in the Bible, in Deuteronomy 22:5, which states that a woman shall not dress as a man, nor shall a man dress as a woman, for whoever does these things is an abomination before God.

The Catholic Church, which set itself up as the absolute representative of christianism, interfered in artistic production and established strict rules of representation. Art, then, had to contribute to the moral edification of society, and the artist was compelled to produce images in which "the sexes could be clearly distinguished, and man could not be confused with women" (Nicolau SEVICENKO, 1996, p. 121).

Despite constant surveillance, some artists defied the canon of representation imposed by the Catholic Church and produced works in which the genders are not completely separated. In many artworks, it is not possible to determine whether the figure portrayed is of the male or female gender, even in religious iconography.

This is what is observed in the work of the Italian Renaissance painter Rafael Sanzio (1483-1520), who in 1503 portrayed St. Sebastian as if he had already ascended to heaven, with no marks of martyrdom or the violent death of which he was the victim.

The portrait shows a figure with bodily features that, by contemporary standards, would be considered feminine. With a face free of facial hair, with thin, high eyebrows, and long, carefully styled hair that cascades down the shoulders, following the same rounded shape of the neck. The hand, which holds the only arrow to indicate that it is St. Sebastian, is small, with thin, delicate fingers.

Not only the face, but also the body of St. Sebastian received, in the hands of various artists - Sandro Botticelli (1474), Alonso Sedano, Carlo Crivelli (1491), Guido Reni (1617), Lorenzo Costa (1491) - a treatment that put his heterosexual cisgender identity under suspicion, being portrayed with features that express femininity.

Michelangelo Merisi Da Caravaggio (1570-1610), one of the most controversial painters of the Italian Baroque period, was bolder in his creations and did not shy away from the impositions of the catholic church. In one of his paintings, portraying Bacchus - the Roman god of wine - his interest in questioning the rigid division of between male and female identities is evident. The young Bacchus's round, smooth face, pouty lips, rosy cheeks, high, carefully drawn eyebrows, sensual gaze, and geisha-like hairstyle, completely distances him from the standard of masculinity of the time.

**FIGURE 6**
Caravaggio, The Young Bacchus,
oil on canvas, 1595
**Source: Page -Vírus da Arte & Cia**[39]

---

[39] Image available at: https://virusdaarte.net/ca-ravaggio-o-jovem-baco/. Accessed July 20, 2021. [E.N.] this link is no longer accessible. The image can be found here at: https://en.wikipedia.org/wiki/Bacchus_%28Caravaggio%29. Last accessed July 14, 2025 at 4:53 pm

Gradually, the trans body found itself distanced from the sacred and the mythological and, as Michel Foucault (1982) explained, became inscribed in the field of monstrification, the pathological and, above all, the obscene, the sinful, the exotic and the criminal.

## Travestis of flesh and blood

One of the rare examples of artistic styles that avoided the hierarchizing of transfeminine bodies can be traced to Japan in the 18th century.

Called "wakashu," female trans people - according to Asato Ikeda (2016), curator of the exhibition A Third Gender: Beautiful Youths in Japanese Prints, which ran from May to November 2016 at the Royal Ontario Museum in Canada - comprised a gender of their own, as defined by biological sex, age, outward appearance, and their role in an established sexual hierarchy.

These youths, biologically male but portrayed as belonging to the female gender by the artists of the Shunga style, were also, in the real world, objects of desire for adult men and women (IKEDA, 2016, n.p.).

The engravings, which are part of the exhibition, explore a social structure and a cultural system that does not fit into a gender binary or even heteronormative sexuality (IKEDA, 2016, n. p.). And it is pertinent to point out that the Shunga style (1600-1868) is characterized by its erotic themes and explicit sexual scenes without any embarrassment.

The artist Shunga portrayed explicit sex scenes in the most varied forms: sex between cis men; sex between cis women; sex between cis men and cis women; sex between cis men and wakashu, between cis women and wakashu, as well as scenes of masturbation, group sex, voyeurism, etc. Among the artists who often reproduced scenes showing wakashu characters are Kitagawa Utamaro (1753-1806), Ishikawa Toyonobu Folio (1711-1785), and Suzuki Harunobu (1724-1770).

As these artists did not make a distinction in the way they portrayed cis women and wakashu, it becomes possible to identify them precisely only in the engravings where the genitals are showing. The entire body structure, hairstyle, gestures, and costumes of these characters follow the same logic of representation as cis characters, confirming and not questioning their feminine identities.

**FIGURE 7**
Suzuki Harunobu, Samurai and His Young Love,
woodcut, 1750
**Source: Pinterest Page[40]**

---

[40] Image available at: https://br.pinterest.com/pin/189854940525316348/. Accessed July 20, 2021. [E.N.] this link no longer works, but the image can be found here:

The delicacy of Harunobu's artwork and the respect for trans identities, including in the titles of his works, is very different from what we see in European art. Even in works depicting well-known personalities, such as Mademoiselle de Beaumont (1728-1810), it is possible to identify very stereotyped narratives.

Known today as the travesti spy of the court of Louis XV, Mademoiselle de Beaumont was portrayed by various artists. In some artworks, the artists' intention to emphasize that this is an exotic, strange, out-of-place body, inscribed in the field of the parodic and painterly, is visible.

These artists include Victor Marie Picot (1744-1805), who, in a 1787 colored engraving, portrayed her during a fencing duel in London, under the astonished gazes of an audience who paid to watch an elderly man, in women's clothing, take on gentlemen from the English court (Tom PAVESI, 2018, n.p.). Thomas Stewart, a successful artist in England who specialized in portraits, painted Mademoiselle de Beaumont in 1792, with a very masculine face and signs of a beard, no breasts, no make-up, and no jewelry.

Another artist, who preferred not to sign his work, produced an even more derogatory image of Mademoiselle de Beaumont. The work, an undated metal engraving, is actually a caricature. The character is standing, facing forward, and looking directly at the viewer. On the left, the character is wearing women's clothing, and on the right side, men's clothing, implying that they are two and not one person.

---

https://en.m.wikipedia.org/wiki/File:Suzuki_Harunobu_Shunga.jpg. Last accessed July 14, 2025.

**FIGURE 8**
Henry R. Robinson, The Man-Monster,
Lithograph, 1836
**Source: Transas City website**[41]

---

[41] Image available at: http://transascity.org/mary-jo-nes-1836/. Accessed July 20, 2021. [E.N.] this link no longer works, but the image can be found here: https://commons.wikimedia.org/wiki/File:Mary_Jones_Lithogram_crop.jpg Last accessed on July 14, 2025.

In all these representations of Mademoiselle de Beaumont, it is not only that the visual narrative leads to a derogatory interpretation, but also the title they received. This statement comes from the fact that they give the persona's civil name, with the not-so-innocent intention of demarcating a social place, suggesting that the female persona was not real. It would be an imitation. A fraud.

Similar forms of representation are identified in other countries.

In the United States of America (USA), in 1836, a color lithograph, signed by Henry R. Robinson, was published in several New York newspapers depicting Mary Jones, a Black travesti prostitute accused of stealing a client's wallet.

Although the image shows Mary Jones elegantly dressed, with a calm countenance and an attitude of relative conformism to the situation imposed on her. The caption refers to her as The Man-Monster, an indication that the feminine outfit, jewelry, makeup, and wig were all part of the disguise she used to attack innocent men. As a potentially dangerous person, she should therefore be kept away from society.

Mary Jones' dehumanization, mainly built through the legal system with the help of journalists and white illustrators, aimed to highlight the fact that "she was someone that the white society feared: Black, gender deviant, sex worker and, probably, the worst of it all, free" (Michael LYONS, 2017, n.p., our translation).

The exposure of Mary Jones is not an isolated case. From the 19th century onwards, with the popularization of printed newspapers and photography,[42] especially in the big cities of England and the USA, there was an increase in the production and dissemination of images of transfeminine

---

[42] Studio portraits self-commissioned by transgender persons are beyond this article's scope.

people with the intention of reaffirming white heterosexual cisgenderness as the only possibility.

**FIGURE 9**
Fanny Park in a cricket game,
glass plate photography, 1869
**Source: Pinterest page**[43]

---

[43] Image available at: https://br.pinterest.com/pin/454441418635851414/. Accessed July 20, 2021.

In April 1870 in London, Fanny Park and Stella Bouton were arrested when they were leaving a theater. The police officer, who had been investigating them for about a year, said: "I have all the reasons to believe that you are men in feminine clothes."

Taken to trial, the Victorian era case caused a scandal. It was a prominent topic in the main newspapers of the English capital.

Fanny and Stella were depicted in different ways, both by illustrators who worked for big newspapers and by illustrators who worked for the police department.

In some images, Fanny and Stella appear being escorted by the police and observed by a curious crowd. In others, they appear in underwear, being forced to get rid of their feminine clothes and replace it with masculine clothes, under the constant watch of police officers.

Different from the images that show Mademoiselle de Beaumont, Fanny and Stella's feminine features are preserved, even if their civil names and their male anatomy were revealed in the reports.

Frances Thompson, Fanny Park, and Stella Bouton had their gender identities questioned, in a violent way, by a society that made efforts to impose and normalize white heterosexual cisgenderness. The images that society tried to make about them gained shape and color at the hands of artists who served this same society.

In contact with other possibilities for bodies and existences, as a rule, the visual arts contributed to monsterizing and pathologizing them, whether through objectifying readings and/or caricatures, or simply by ignoring them.

## Two spirits or more in the Americas

Cynara Menezes (2016) objectively asks: "How else did Europeans contribute to the sexuality of the Americas besides introducing us to guilt?" (MENEZES, 2016, n.p., our translation)

The domination process imposed by Europe, not by chance, paid great attention to the religious practices of the colonized peoples. Considered pagans, they needed to be quickly replaced by christianism.

Eliminating religious diversity implied the elimination of sexual freedom and gender diversity, expressed in rituals led by shamans that challenged cisgender norms, as identified in the "Aztec, Chimu, Lacke, Lubaca, Manta, Maia, Mbaya, Moche and Tupinambá" cultures (JONES, 2006, our translation). Menezes (2016) goes beyond this and affirms that trans people, feminine and masculine, were found in more than 150 tribes, in North America alone.

Called Two-Spirit or Berdaches, Peter Jones (2007) explains that they performed special tasks, being responsible for taking care of children and passing on teachings and myths to them. As they saw the world through both men's and women's eyes, they could predict the future, which is why they were considered the most suitable for shamanic activities.

As religious leaders, the Berdaches would have mediating roles "not only between men and women, but also between the physical and the spiritual." (Walter L. WILLIAMS, 2012, n.p., our translation).

According to Stefan Zebrowski-Rubin (2009), the term Berdache would have "an extremely derogatory connotation, derived from the ancient French word bardache, which means prostitute, gay or passive sodomite" (RUBIN, 2009, n.p. My translation).

Despite the prejudiced attitude through which the European invader treated the Two-Spirit culture, being described in a negative way or simply being ignored, it did not disappear completely and was mainly preserved by remnants of the Navajo, Cheyenne, and Cherokee tribes in the United States of America.

One of the few artists to register elements of the Two-Spirit culture was the American George Catlin (1796-1872), who produced an extensive iconographic record of many original populations that inhabited part of the territory of the current USA.

Regarding the Two-Spirit culture, Catlin stated that it was one of the most inexplicable and disgusting customs that he had known, and he wished for it to become extinct before it was recorded more completely (RUBIN, 2009, n.p., my translation).

**FIGURE 10**
George Catlin, Dance to the Berdache
Saukie, 1861-1869, oil on card

**Source: SAAM page[44]**

George Catlin's opinion, however violent it may seem, translates the thinking of a time and of a society.

---

[44] Image available at: https://americanart.si.edu/artwork/dance-berdash-4023. Accessed July 14, 2025.

In an interview with Cynara Menezes (2016), an anthropologist and professor at the University of Rondônia, Estevão Fernandes explains that:

> [...] men should dress as men, work where men work, have a man's name, and behave as men do; the same regarding women. The Indigenous people who did not fit this (re)strictive perspective on sexual dimorphism and heteronormativity were punished— there are reports, for example, of executions, forced haircuts, physical punishment, etc., carried out by the colonizers (MENEZES, 2016, n.p., our translation).

It is possible to suppose that the artists' decisions—who worked on the American continent, many in the service of European governments— not to portray trans people were associated with the punishments described by Fernandes (2016). This was precisely because such people were considered less than human, even subjected to the death penalty.

When these registries were done—as it happened with Two-Spirits at the end of the 19th century, photographed in improvised studios in poses determined by the photographer—they ought to have reinforced the idea that they needed, urgently, to go through a civilizatory process, in the molds imposed by the European invader, so that they would display attitudes compatible with their anatomy.

In other regions of the American continent, as in Brazil, for example, what is seen is an absolute silence regarding trans people. Even if they were a part of the daily life of Brazilian society, especially among the Black population, as Jocélio Teles dos Santos (1996) attests in Salvador and Nina Raymundo Rodrigues (2010) in Rio de Janeiro.

## Some considerations

The images, as Manguel (2001) states, allow several readings beyond those that consider aesthetic values such as balance, volume, rhythm, symmetry/asymmetry, construct, tensions, line, colors, depth, light and shadow, moment, rigidity, texture, proportion, space, etc. They also make it possible for other readings to take place and thus to question to what extent these same aesthetic values align with others (like form, gesture, language, composition, ambiance, among others). They are values used to build discourses that reinforce or challenge hierarchies, exclusions, stereotypes, and/or prejudice (OLIVEIRA, 2020, our translation).

Analyzing the forms of representation of transfeminine bodies in the visual arts until the 19th century, in different cultures across the Asian, African, and American continents, points to diverse possibilities, given that the most recurring situation in all cultures was silence. A silence that cannot exactly reflect how the artistic production of these peoples was before the contact with Europe, especially because it was the European, heterosexual, cisgender, white man who decided what should be preserved, remembered, and celebrated.

Therefore, the gaze I have, regarding the visual arts, is not exempt from a European masculinist intervention, even though I make an effort to look from another place. Because "there is great value in defining the possibility of seeing from the periphery and the abysses" (HARAWAY, 1995, p. 22, our translation).

This silence that interferes with the process of identifying the artworks, which portray transfeminine bodies, is one of the numerous forms in which transphobia is expressed. It is a "power device" (FOUCALT, 1979, our translation), because it operates to impose white heterosexual cisgenderness as the only possibility of existence.

According to Peter Jones' reflections (2006), gender identities different from cisgenderness, he calls "poligender," would be a result of politeism: behind several sexual choices there would be the belief in numerous gods, directly influencing artistic production, as it happened in Rome, Greece, and Africa before the contact with christianism.[45]

The control exercised by christianism, in Europe and in the colonies, did not only interfere in artistic production, but also in the relationship we have with the art that preceded it, compromising our aesthetic and discursive interpretation.

Not by chance, in Europe and in the Americas, the artistic production that portrayed bodies and sexual practices considered sinful "were hidden, locked in museum rooms until the middle of the 20th century" (MENEZES, 2016, n.p., our translation), hidden away from the general public.

The art that previously celebrated bodies considered holy, like Dogon's sculpture in Mali, was used to reaffirm cultural, racial, and gender hierarchies when it was classified as primitive and/or pagan. By inferiorizing Dogon art, the Europeans, with the help of the church, medicine, and law, attempted to inferiorize the bodies that it depicted. Transfeminine bodies, then, are displaced from the holy field and placed in a sinful, pathological, and dangerous one, the one needing to be eliminated.

Shunga art, in Japan, away from christianism's control, kept depicting transfeminine bodies without, apparently, hierarchizing them in relation to cis bodies.

In England and in the United States of America, the few examples of images portraying transfeminine people, especially in the 19th century, worked in favor of cisgender normalization.

It is not about holding artists accountable or excusing them from productions full of prejudice and stereotypes, especially because, as the research showed, they were in a context where they had limited control over

---

[45] Peter Jones posits in his argument that sexual orientation is a choice, akin to gender identity, and both are linked to religious practices.

their work. This control was even less when they produced works on commission, as was the case with illustrators and photographers.

Inexplicably, some of the stereotypes identified in 19th-century artistic production are present in contemporary academic works, which refuse conceptual revisionism and insist on using terms that contribute to exoticizing and hierarchizing transfeminine people.

My goal with this article, by bringing discursive fragments about the presence and the absence of travestis and/or trans women in the visual arts, is to draw attention to a normative power, present not only in artistic productions from the past, but mainly in the studies that address it nowadays.

To break with this situation, I believe it is necessary to dialogue with other areas of knowledge, such as ethnic-racial studies, gender and sexual diversity studies, and transfeminist studies.

I also believe that debates like this can contribute to the reassessment of, and fight against, prejudiced views regarding travestis and/or trans women, so that we can build a heterogeneous society. A society in which the practice of respect is in fact a reality based on, as Haraway (1995) suggests, contestation, deconstruction, network connections, and the hope for the transformation of knowledge systems and ways of seeing.

## REFERENCES

AGUIAR, Rodrigo Simas. **Arte Rupestre: conceitos introdutórios**, 2012. Available at: http://www.rupestreweb.info/introduccion.html. Last accessed September 1, 2025.

AILEEN AJOOTIAN. **The Only Happy Couple: Hermaphrodites and Gender**. p. 220-42. In: LYON, C.; KOLOSKI-STROW, A.O. Naked Truths. London and New York: Routledge, 2004.

BERBARA, Maria; FONSECA, Raphael. **De Akhenaton a Duchamp: arte, transexualismo e androginia**, 2011. Available at:

http://www.anpap.org.br/anais/2011/pdf/chtca/maria_louro_berbara.pdf. Last accessed April 20, 2020.

DUSSEL, Inés; CARUSO, Marcelo. **A invenção da sala de aula: uma genealogia das formas de ensinar**. São Paulo: Moderna, 2003; p. 103–156.

FOUCAULT. M.1 **Herculine Barbin: o diário de um hermafrodita**. Rio de Janeiro: Francisco Alves, 1982.

GUILHERME FILHO, Jair. **Itinerário, estudo estético e estilístico de uma escultura Dogon: "figura hermafrodita" do mestre de Yayé**. Thesis. Masters in Aesthetics. São Paulo University, 2014.

IKEDA, Asato. **A Third Gender: Beautiful Youths in Japanese Prints**, 2016. Available at: https://enfilade18thc.com/2016/05/09/exhibition-a-third-gender-beautiful-youths-in-japanese-prints/ . Last accessed May 4, 2020.

JONES, Peter. **O Deus do Sexo: como a espiritualidade define a sua sexualidade**. São Paulo: Editora Cultura Cristã, 2007.

HARAWAY, Donna. **Saberes Localizados: a questão da ciência para o feminismo e o privilégio da perspectiva parcial**. Cadernos Pagu, n. 5, p. 7-41, 1995.

LEULOP, Hélene. **Dogon**. Paris. Somogy Éditions d'Art. Musée du Quai Branly, 2011.

LOPES, Anchyses Jobim. **Transexualidades – psicanálise e mitolo gia grega**. Estudos de Psicanálise, Belo Horizonte-MG, n.47, p. 47–72, jul. 2017.

LYONS, Michael. **Mary Jones, Patron Saint of the Scam**, 2017. Available at: https://www.dailyxtra.com/mary-jones-patron-saint-of--the-scam-72972 . Last accessed October 14, 2019.

MANGUEL, Alberto. **Lendo imagens**. São Paulo: Companhia das Letras, 2001.

MENEZES, Cynara. **Como a Igreja arruinou a vida sexual das Amé ricas com pecado, culpa e preconceito**, 2016. Available at:

https://www.geledes.org.br/como-igreja-arruinou-vida-sexual-das-americas-com-pecado-culpa-e-preconceito/. Last accessed May 4, 2020.

OLIVEIRA, Megg Rayara Gomes de. **Divas, Divinas e Poderosas: Fragmentos discursivos a respeito da presença de travestis e mulheres transexuais no campo do sagrado,** 2019. Available at: https://peita.me/blogs/putablog/divas-divinas-e-poderosas-fragmentos-discursivos-a-respeito-da-presenca-de-travestis-e-mulheres-transexuais-no-campo-do-sagrado?srsltid=AfmBOooHBsmyeWF4-gTI4W_MPstqr1RfoPYnIR45CaARYlwbzaUY7pKJo. Last accessed September 1, 2025.

OLIVEIRA, Megg Rayara Gomes de. Sim, Eu Aceito! Conjugalidade, casamento e organização familiar negra durante o regime escravista no Brasil. Revista ARTE FILOSOFIA, v. 15 n. 28, p. 4-23, 2020: Dossiê Estética Africana. Available at: https://periodicos.ufop.br/raf/article/view/3969. Last accessed September 1, 2025.

OLIVEIRA, Megg Rayara Gomes de. Transexistências negras: o lugar de travestis e mulheres transexuais negras no Brasil e em África até o século XIX. p. 69–88. In: RIBEIRO, Paula Regina Costa... [et al.]. **Corpo, gênero e sexualidade: resistências e ocupa(ações) nos espaços de educação**. Rio Grande: Ed. Da FURG, 2018.

PAVESI, Tom. **O travesti espião no reinado de Luís XV,** 2018. Available at: https://segredosdeparis.com/o-travesti-espiao-no-reinado-de-luis-xv/. Last accessed September 1, 2025.

RODRIGUES, Raymundo Nina. **Os africanos no Brasil**. Rio de Janeiro: Centro Edelstein de Pesquisas Sociais, 2010.

SANFELICE, Pérola de Paula. **A Arte do Corpo: incorporando a sexualidade masculina e feminina na cultura material de Pompéia,** 2013. Available at https://portaldeperiodicos.animaeducacao.com.br/index.php/memorare_grupep/article/view/1883> Last accessed September 1, 2025.

SANTOS, Ana Lúcia Fonseca. **Um sexo que são vários: a (im) pos sibilidade do intersexo,** 2012. https://estudogeral.sib.uc.pt/handle/10316/20210. . Last accessed September 1, 2025.

SANTOS, Jean Carlo Silva dos. **Masculinidades, feminilidades e an droginia: uma análise interpretativa sobre a construção social de gêneros e suas implicações para o exercício da liderança no Poder Judiciário de Rondônia**. Dissertation. PHD in Administration. Universidade Federal do Rio Grande do Sul, 2013.

SANTOS, Jocélio Teles dos. **Incorrigíveis, afeminados, desenfrea dos: indumentária e travestismo na Bahia do século XIX**.Revista de Antropologia, v.40, n.2, São Paulo, 1997. Available at: https://revistas.usp.br/ra/article/view/27056/28828. Last accessed September 1, 2025.

SEVCENKO, Nicolau. **As Alegorias da experiência marítima e a construção do europocentrismo**. In: SCHWARCZ, Lilia Moritz; QUEIROZ, Renato da Silva (Org.). Raça e Diversidade. São Paulo: EDUSP, 1996.

SILVA, Alberto da Costa e. **A enxada e a lança: a África antes dos portugueses**. Rio de Janeiro: Nova Fronteira, 2006.

SILVA, Paulo Vinicius Baptista da. **Projeto "Racismo e discurso na América Latina": notas sobre personagens negras e brancas no discurso midiático brasileiro**. In: III Simpósio Internacional sobre Análise do Discurso, Belo Horizonte, Núcleo de Análise do Discurso (NAD) e o Programa de Pós-Graduação da Faculdade de Letras da Universidade Federal de Minas Gerais, 1º a 4 de abril de 2008.

VERGER, Pierre. **Notas sobre o culto aos orixás e voduns na Bahia de todos os santos, no Brasil e na antiga costa de escravos na África**. São Paulo: EDUSP, 1999.

VIEIRA, Fernanda Dantas. A caça aos homossexuais e às travestis na ditadura militar. Pragmatismo Político, 2015. Available at: https://www.pragmatismopolitico.com.br/2015/04/a-caca-aos-homossexuais-e-travestis-na-ditadura-militar.html. Last accessed August 8, 2018.

VIGOYA, Mara Viveros. **La interseccionalidad: una aproximación situada a la dominación**. Debate Feminista, v. 52, p. 1-17, out., 2016. Available at: http://www.sciencedirect.com/science/article/pii/S0188947816300603. Last accessed July 24, 2017.

WILLAMS, Walter L. **A tradição Berdache**. Available in English at: https://faculty.sfcc.spokane.edu/InetShare/AutoWebs/SarahMa/williams%20the%20berdache%20tradition.pdf. Last accessed September 1, 2025.

A escultura de Pan e Hermafrodita não consegue encontrar um comprador. **WORDPRESS**. 10 jun. 2011, n.p. Available at: https://latunicadeneso.wordpress.com/2011/06/10/. Last accessed September 1, 2025.

ZEBROWSKI-RUBIN, Stefan. **Dance of Two Spirits—Kent Monkman at Montreal's Museum of Fine Arts**, 2009. Available at: https://www.theartblog.org/2009/08/dance-of-two-spirits-kent-monkman-at--montreals-museum-of-fine-arts/. Last accessed May 4, 2020.

# 4

# CANDOMBLE:
## A PLACE OF RESISTANCE AND STRUGGLE FOR CITIZENSHIP AND RELIGIOUS FREEDOM FOR TRANS WOMEN AND TRAVESTIS[46]

### Fernanda de Moraes da Silva[47]
### Translated from Brazilian Portuguese by Bruna Barros

> *One of the world creation myths tells that Odúdúwa is its creator, founder, and Ilé-Ifè's first Obá Òóni, the progenitor of all Yorùbá people.*
> —Aulo Barreti Filho, Ilê-Ifè, the Origin of the World, 1983

## Introduction

For quite some time, Trans Women and Travestis have been considering and re-analyzing social and anthropological education as a space for action, and a strategic place for action against religious intolerance, social

---

[46] [T.N.] Travesti is a transfeminine identity in Brazil. See Barros, Bruna and Jess Oliveira. 2020. "Black Sapatão Translation Practices: Healing Ourselves a Word Choice at a Time." *Caribbean Review of Gender Studies*, Issue 14: 43–52.

[47] Fernanda de Moraes da Silva is an Ìyálórìṣà (Candomblé Ketu), theologian, social worker, and activist. holds a postgraduate degree in Human Rights and Sexuality and is the General Executive Secretary of ANTRA (National Association of Travestis and Transsexuals); State Coordinator of FONATRANS (National Forum of Black Travestis and Transsexuals) in São Paulo; and President of Aphrodite Institute (Organized Group for the Promotion of Social Inclusion and Citizenship for Transexuals and Travestis).

inequalities, and transphobic racism. Such analyzes shows that, within this religious setting, an educational model based on Western civilizational values is reproduced under a hegemonic cisnormative perspective, denying the sexual and gender diversity that exists in Brazilian society. In other words, there is the reinforcement of an ideology that refuses and demeans transsexualities and travestilities,[48] which are present in the daily life of these cults. This practice notably escalates when associated with other social markers, such as class, race, and ethnicity.

This article seeks to contribute to such reflections. It is the result of a brief review of transsexuality, travestility, or trans identities in the various houses of worship of African diasporic religions, and of scholarship on the importance of Trans Women and Travestis in the constitution of African-Brazilian religiosity. The presence of Trans Women and Travestis within Candomblé Houses, whether as *Ìyálórìṣàs*[49] or as *Ómó Òrìṣà* (daughter of the santo),[50] equally represents the strength of Candomblé as a religion that reclaims Black trans identity in Brazil.

The spaces presented here are located in the city of São Paulo; more precisely, in the Candomblé Houses[51] whose representation, within the

---

[48] [T.N.] The author uses "transsexual" and "transsexualidade[s]" in Brazilian Portuguese. I chose to use both "trans"—a more current and widely used term to refer to trans identities—and "transsexual"—when the author is referring to herself, to respect the specific way she uses the term to address her own identity. Furthermore, I translated "transsexualidade[s]" as "transsexuality[ies]" and "travestilidade[s]"—which refers to travesti identities — as "travestility[ies]." These terms are at times capitalized by the author as a way to add emphasis.

[49] [T.N.]Popularly called *mães de santo* in Brazil. A mother of [the] saint[s], a mother of Òrìsá, a Candomblé priestess.

[50] [T.N.]Popularly called *filhas de santo* in Brazil. A daughter of [the] saint[s], a daughter of Òrìsá, a Candomblé initiate.

[51] [T.N./E.N.] A Candomblé House is also referred to as *Ilé Àṣẹ* (Yoruba) or *terreiro/terreiro de Candomblé* (Brazilian Portuguese) or *Casas de Àṣẹ* (Àṣẹ Houses). [E.N.] While the term santo literally means saint as in a Christian context, there is one way that the term "saint" as understood by English speaking Christinan practitioners, is not translatable when representing

*terreiro* environment, is a specific Òrìṣà/Nkisi/Vodun which represents practitioners' way of living and socializing as a whole. Within Candomblé hierarchies, rituals are revered and carried out according to the specifications of these Houses, which hold specific combinations of qualities, characteristics, precepts, doctrines, and teachings acquired through their experiences and the heritage left by our ancestors from the African continent.

## Candomblé—An African-Brazilian Religion

The term *"candomblé"* is a combination of the Kimbundu term *"candombe"* (dance with atabaques) and the Yorùbá term *"Ilé"* (house): it therefore means "house of dance with atabaques." Candomblé is a religion that derives from African animism, and it involves the worship of Òrìṣà, Vodun, or Nkisi—denominations given to the *"incorporated entities"* (popularly used term) in the Candomblé religious practice. Such denominations vary according to the African nation from which the practices of each Candomblé House derive. Totemic and familiar, it is one of the most practiced African diasporic religions, having more than three million adherents and followers around the world, mainly in Brazil.

Among the African nations that practice animism, each one has worshiped only a single Òrìṣà (or Vodun or Nkisi). The joining of cults is a

---

the way it has been appropriated by practitioners of African-Based religious traditions in the Americas. In fact, those who practice the religion in English speaking countries, we either use Òrìṣà/Nkisi/Vodun - depending on the house (religious lineage) the practitioner is from, OR if the person is from a house that has its origins in Latin America or the Spanish Speaking Caribbean, practitioners rarely use the word "Saint." Practitioners typically use the Spanish or Portuguese word "Santo." Using the word "saint," in the English translation doesn't reflect that whenever people in the religion use "santo," everyone knows is meant - an Òrìṣà/Nkisi/Vodun - within an Afro-diasporic religious context. In this translation we have agreed on using "santo" as it points to a very specific type of epistemic (r)existence present in the word's contextual usage.

Brazilian phenomenon[52], and it happened as a result of the trafficking of African peoples who were enslaved in Brazil. Grouped together in *senzalas*,[53] different African ethnic groups appointed a person to care for the Òrìsà, also known as *Ìyálórìsà*, in the case of women, and as *Babálórìsà*, in the case of men.

The religion is based on the anima (soul) of Nature and is therefore called anemic. The African priestesses and priests who were trafficked and enslaved in Brazil brought along their Black gods, called Òrìsà/Nkisi/Vodun, their culture, and their languages. Between 1549 and 1888, they tried, in one way or another, to continue practicing their religions in Brazilian lands. African peoples implemented their religions in Brazil, bringing together several cults in a single house of worship to ensure their survival.

The African-Brazilian religion, generically called **Candomblé** (*place of worship for the Black population*), and of African (*Ìbere*) origin, means "dance." It is seen as a religious dance in which people pray and invoke, as one of the forms of worshiping and believing in the Òrìsà. Òrìsà means energy, strength—nature itself in its variations, nuances of beauty, and devastation. Therefore, it is correct to say that Candomblé is a ritualistic dance that worships nature in its most diverse forms. In the case of Brazil, Candomblé emerged historically as a focus of cultural-religious resistance by Black and disadvantaged populations to preserve their histories (*Ìtàns*), traditions, and the fundamental elements of their set of beliefs.

Òrìsà have individual personalities, skills, and ritual preferences. They are connected to the specific natural phenomena: Fire, Earth, Air, and

---

[52] E.N.] Please note the joining of cults is quite common thorough out the Americas. This was not changed in the text as we respect the experience and the positionality of the author.

[53] [T.N.] Slave quarters on plantations.

Water. Each person is chosen at birth (*Ìbí*) by one or more "patrons" called Òrìṣà, through which an *Ìyálórìṣà* or *Babálórìṣà* will identify them.

Some Òrìṣà "possess" initiates during the Candomblé ritual; some Òrìṣà do not, they are only worshiped in trees by the community. Some Òrìṣà called Fúnfún (white) Òrìṣà, which were part of the creation of the world, also possess adherents. Conceptually, we start from the idea of "Òrìṣàísm understood as: a set of religions or the religion of those who worship the Yorùbá Òrìṣà. We are, then, Òrìṣàísts" (Berreti Filho, 1983, 4-5).

Including all nations, Candomblé reveres around fifty of the hundreds of deities still worshiped in Africa. However, in most Candomblé Houses in large cities, there are twelve who are the most worshiped. Some deities have "qualities" that can be "identified" in their characteristics and worshiped under different names. In each Candomblé House, they can be called: Òrìṣà (Ketu), Nkisi (Angola), or Vodun (Jeje). Thus, the list of deities from different nations is long, and each nation is different from the other; their cults, rituals, and songs are totally different.

A possible definition for Candomblé by Maria Salete Joaquim is:

> Candomblé is the religion of *Àṣẹ*. When we call life, we go back to our origins. Candomblé is a celebration of this life, of Olódùmarè, who is present in our struggle and history; dancing, singing, and eating with people. Òrìṣà walk with people (Joaquim, 2001, p. 78).

Candomblé is, in its composition, a community with a diverse cultural heritage within which many elements are mixed, most of them African.[54]

In Brazil, historically, Candomblé has been a place that shelters minorities who seek acceptance. It is also a religion with a very peculiar hierarchy, codes, and symbolism. It is important that, based on this

---

[54] [E.N.] Candomblé is also influenced by Indigenous practices from the Hemisphere.

diversity, Candomblé can welcome people as they present themselves in society: that is, according to the Gender Identity they present, without the need for "conversion" to certain value judgments or "social adjustments."

The ritualistic community (*Egbé*) of Candomblé determines for each person their own place, and no person is left with no place within this human amalgam. Because women and men, whether cis or trans, have very well-defined positions and functions in such communities, it is not allowed for certain positions established for women to be held by men and/or vice versa. However, considering the discussions about sexual and gender expressions, what about Trans Women and Travestis initiated into Candomblé Houses?

## Initiation and Priesthood

Knowing yourself: a basic prerequisite for personal fulfillment at all spiritual levels. Since their origin, human beings have longed to meet the Infinite. This tireless search often generates certain battles, which are fought within the individual, along with feelings of anguish, anxiety, nonconformity, or even despair in the face of the unknown or the inevitable: the fatalities and uncertainties of tomorrow, the cycle of life, fate, and death.

A person with mediumship carries an ancestral weight in this matter. We are the sum of the consciousness of our ancestors, so we carry in our DNA an ancestral memory, heritages, debts, suffering, joys, wisdom, and even their personalities. What attests to this context is the fact that we are similar to our parents, grandparents, and great-grandparents; that is, we are similar to our most distant ancestors, the Òrìṣà/Nkisi/Vodun. And this ancestrality is loaded with responsibilities and burdens.

I was initiated into Candomblé (*Igbódù Òrìṣà*) at Ilè Àṣẹ de Oyá Topè, in Manaus, Amazonas, Brazil, in February 1993, and received my priesthood, my position as *Ìyálóriṣà*, at Ilè Àṣẹ Odé Ópá Óká, in Rio de Janeiro, in 2010, by my *Babálóriṣà* Gilmar Pereira, *Fomo de Yèmójá*, (Babá

Sesú Toyan). I was chosen and graced by the Òrìṣà to occupy this position. And, although I do not wish to delve into controversy and/or make personal provocations and questionings, as a *Ìyálórìṣà* and as a Transsexual Woman, I could not omit myself or fail to do my analysis.

Throughout my journey, I have invited my *Agbás* (elders) and my Àṣẹ Òrìṣà family (*Ebí*) to discuss and reflect on a subject that society, in different spaces and in many studies, has considered: the issue of transsexuality. However, within Candomblé and other older African-Brazilian religions, which are always only seen as traditional and matriarchal religions, little has been reflected and discussed on the topic of (trans)sexualities. Well, transsexualities or travestilities possess their particularities as well as the peculiarities that are specific to each person; they cannot be taken as a reference in the initiation of a *Yáwò*.[55]

Gender categorizations are created as a cisnormative society determines, following standards created by men or religions. However, how do we define transsexualities and travestilities within African diasporic religions? We invariably stumble upon cases that do not fit the models of cisnormative society, made in the "image" of God (Olódùmarè), who, in all its manifestations, adds masculine and feminine elements at the same time.

Transsexualities and travestilities have no space in this intolerant cisnormative society, which tries to suppress and extinguish the feminine characteristics of trans women and travestis. They struggle in different ways, whether through their clothing or the exercise of their freedom to occupy a position as Ìyás (mothers) within the religious context, or against superstitious, cisnormative, biology-centered, enslaving, pathologizing, and reductionist oppressions, offering arguments and contextualization about how trans women and travestis should be treated. These "struggles" tend to

---

[55] [T.N.] Yáwò is an initiate who is possessed by Òrìṣà in Candomblé Ketu.

take on the appearance of common and even respectful actions. For we do not want to separate and segregate Candomblé between specific groups of people; an example of this would be the emergence of new Candomblé Houses led, managed, and attended only by trans women or travestis, since we are a unique sisterhood, although spread throughout the Brazilian territory.

However, this is not the case in Òrìsàism, because the deities, that is, the Òrìsà, are indifferent to a person's gender identity, as long as they have a good character (*Iwá Pèlé*). There is a Yoruba proverb that says: *Ayanmó ni Iwá Pèlé, Iwá Pèlé ni ayanmó*. Roughly translated, this proverb means: *[One's] fate is [one's] good character, [one's] good character is [one's] fate.*

If, in African-Brazilian cults, faith determines that the head (*Orí*)—as a principle of individuation and object of worship, of religiosity—commands and carries the body (*Árá*), how can we demand that a person who is assigned a sex at birth that is incongruous with their birth gender, but suited to another gender, perform, dress and behave in our rituals according to a biology-centered reductionist "assignment"? In oral tradition, myths bring our ancestors' understanding of various issues that intrigue humanity. And, with a more accurate interpretation, myths can be the route that will help us not only accept and welcome these people as they are, but, above all, to respect their real gender identity, their desires, and their beliefs.

Therefore, a trans woman or a travesti (a person who was assigned male at birth, but who changed her body and social identity to the female gender and lives that way on a daily basis), for example, may dress as a *baiana*, in feminine attire, and occupy a position consistent with their current gender. In this sense, Milton Silva dos Santos maintains that:

> In the mystical union constituted between the Òrìsà and their double, prevails the sacred and non-biological nature of the relationship commitment between them. The initiated man is

not a sexual being during possession. He does not lose his masculinity because, at that moment, it is not he who is present, but the Òrìṣà to which he was initiated. There is no sexual contradiction; after all, it is the divinity who dresses in ritual clothing in order to perform liturgical choreographies (Santos, 2008, p. 6).

Behavior must be determined by the gender identity presented, that is, by what the person actually is (and, why not, it is their right), and not by what others think or believe that person to be, highlighting the political dimension between Candomblé and the expressions of transsexualities.

## Trans Identities within Candomblé Houses

Transsexualities or travestilities are present in the majority of Candomblé Houses throughout Brazil. However, they are hidden and, indisputably, camouflaged or "overlooked" by principle and, often, denied by many *Ìyálórìṣàs* or *Babálórìṣàs*, who deny their daughters of santo who are trans women or travestis to dress accordingly to their gender identity.

In Candomblé, transsexualities and travestilities are widely accepted, but not often discussed nowadays. However, there was a time when trans women and *travestis* could not be initiated as *"rodantes"* (term used for people who go into trance with the Òrìṣà). Sometimes they were also not allowed in Candomblé, because they were seen as homosexual men and, if they danced in the *Xirè* (Candomblé circle dance), even if they were in a trance, some people said it was an affront to the elder matriarchs.

Trans women and *travestis*, when uncomfortable with not feeling like they belong to their birth sex/gender, seek intense body modifications. These procedures include hormone replacement therapy, the injection of industrial liquid silicone—in the case of *travestis* and trans women; others have plastic surgeries. Usually, they find in these methods, some of which are illegal, a more attractive way, from a cis-aesthetic point of view, of adapting body and mind. That is why they cannot hide their true gender identity behind screens or inside social "closets." This "(in)visibility" is nearly mandatory, from the moment they decide to come out publicly and socially.

And, for those [transmasculine and transfeminine] in which the fluidity, the associations, and the conflicts between these socially and politically constructed and constituted "identities" are inscribed on the body—as a stigmatizing remnant of their assigned gender which cannot be omitted under any cisnormative disguise—the prejudice (transphobia) and violence that they suffer in their daily lives are even greater. Trans women and *travestis* are not effeminate gay men, or people who merely dress like women, because, socially, politically, and psychologically, they already are [women].

In traditional Yorùbá culture, the *Orí* (head) can lead to an opening for the topic of transsexuality, considering that an *Orí* may or may not carry a gender identity with it; however, if it brings it from *Òrún*, we could infer that the Òrìṣà are indifferent to the transsexualities and travestilities of their *Ómó Òrìṣà*.

In Candomblé Houses, it is well established among *Ìyálóriṣàs* and *Babálóriṣàs* that a person's gender does not change with the trance of the Òrìṣà (*èlègún*), whether *Ayágbás* (the female Òrìṣà) or *Ógbórós* (the male Òrìṣà), since the initiated person (*Yáwò*) does not find themselves, on the occasion of the trance, as a sexual being but rather as someone "inhabited," that is, incorporated, by the sacred presence of Òrìṣà. Thus, we can consider that transsexualities and travestilities do not affect a person's spirituality or faith, once we establish that Òrìṣà do not discriminate, nor do they have any prejudice towards anyone's gender or gender identity.

If a trans woman or a travesti holds a position within a Candomblé House, how will they be accepted and seen? Will they be considered *Ìyálóriṣàs* or *Babálóriṣàs*? Their assigned gender is not consistent with the Gender Identity that the person presents, that is, a Trans Woman or a

Travesti has feminine gender. So, what is there to do with these people within the hierarchy of Candomblé Òrìṣàism?

Since Candomblé accepts people with their dreams, aspirations, idiosyncrasies, characteristics, particularities, and neuroses—in short, in the condition they present themselves—a Trans Woman or a Travesti should be able to be a *Ìyálórìṣà* — for this person is uncomfortable with their assigned gender and does not accept themself in the category of the biology-centered, reductionist cisnormative condition.

Why would we do the opposite and attack them with a position or role in the Candomblé House that does not match their real Gender Identity? The Òrìṣà do not limit themselves to sexualities; they include and accept our needs more than any human being. A position in a Candomblé House, first of all, is offered and blessed by Òrìṣà. Let us comprehend that these beautiful energies, which are the Òrìṣà, would never negatively affect a person in the beautiful, luminous, and important moment of being granted a position. The Òrìṣà/Nkisi/Vodun are intermediate deities; along with Òlòrún, they provide spiritual support to the *Ómó Òrìṣàs*, and govern the world and human beings. But they are also part of this world as elements of nature; part of humanity as mythical ancestors; and part of each human being as components of their personality.

Candomblé is the religion of *Asé*. When we evoke life, we evoke the ancestralities of our Òrìṣà. Therefore, the worship of the Òrìṣà in Candomblé, whether in the initiation process or in our religious obligations, is the promotion and celebration of a person's life, of Òlódùmarè, who is present in our struggle and history: dancing, singing, eating, and walking with people. In Candomblé, deities have human attributes, virtues, and flaws; and the adherents have, in turn, divine characteristics—since, in addition to being *Ómó Òrìṣàs*, we carry our Orí (head); that is, a deity that protects our path and our fate.

The sacred language used in Candomblé Houses derives from the Yorùbá or Nagô language. The people of *Asé* try to remain faithful to the teachings of their African ancestors, who founded the first Houses, and reenact their rituals, prayers, traditions, songs, food, and festivals. All of these teachings are passed on orally to this day. According to Júlio Braga:

> Candomblé is, in essence, a community with a diverse cultural heritage, where elements from West Africa and Brazil are mixed. Due to the relationships to which they have been permanently subjected, many other religious components of different origins are also integrated. Due to its internal dynamics and the sense of religiosity that is present at all moments of community life, Candomblé is a constant generator of ethical and behavioral values that enrich and leave its mark on the country's cultural heritage (Braga, 1998, p. 37).

In Candomblé, there is no idea of sin, hell, or purgatory. This, however, does not imply a permissive or reductionist existence. The reference point for life is life itself, since its essence and composition take place on two parallel planes: in the *ayè* (world) and in the *òrún* (beyond). Thus, each material element has its double spiritual and abstract meaning in the *òrún*, and each component in the *òrún* has its material aspect in the *ayè*.

## Final Considerations

This essay represents a new opening for African-Brazilian religions in the face of identity struggles and the representation of social movements, organized by trans women and *travestis*, spread throughout Brazil and around the world. This opening takes place amidst a context in which issues linked to transsexuality and travestility are an immense taboo in most religions, if not openly condemned.

Despite considering the experiences of non-cisgender sexualities, transsexualities, and travestilities as a "mortal error" (*aíe apáníyan*), movements against this view are emerging in several Candomblé Houses throughout Brazil. Although there are some important figures from Candomblé who are thinking about sexual morality within African-Brazilian religions, the need to rethink such concepts is also recognized. The non-religious have been gaining prominence in these issues with the creation of groups such as ANTRA (Brazilian National Association of *Travestis* and Transsexuals) and FONATRANS (Brazilian National Forum of Black Travestis and Transsexuals). The movement of Candomblé adherents has sought to provide support to trans women and *travestis*, while at the same time seeking to promote and include acceptance and respect for this population in the agenda of Candomblé Houses.[56]

## REFERENCES

BERRETI Filho, Aulo. **Nações Africanas: Miscigenação nos Candomblés do Brasil.** Revista Ébano, nº 19, p. 4-5, 1983.

BRAGA, Júlio. **Fuxico do candomblé: estudos afro-brasileiros.** Feira de Santana: UEFS, 1998.

JOAQUIM, Maria Salete. **O papel da liderança religiosa feminina na construção da identidade negra.** Rio de Janeiro: Pallas, 2001.

LIMA, Vivaldo da Costa. **A família de santos nos candomblés Jejê-Nagô da Bahia: um estudo de relações intergrupais.** Bahia, Master's thesis, UFBA, 1977.

---

[56] This article was originally published on January 29, 2019, on ANTRAS's website: https://antrabrasil.org/2019/01/29/candomble-um-ambiente-de-resistencia-e-luta-pelo-liberdade-cidada-e-culto-religioso-da-populacao-das-mulheres-transexuais-e-das-travestis/. Accessed July 20, 2021. Its publication in this collection was authorized by da Silva.

SANTOS, Milton Silva dos. "Mito, possessão e sexualidade no candomblé." **Revista Nures**, n. 8, p. 1-9. PUC-SP, 2008.

# 5

# QUILOMBO MANDATA:
## BLACK TRAVESTIS DISPUTING POLITICAL INSTITUTIONALITY[57]

Erica Malunguinho[58]
Maria Clara Araújo dos Passos[59]
Translated by Flávia Kunsch

"Our steps come from afar"[60]

---

[57] [T. N.] According to Catraca Livre, Erica Malunguinho refers to her mandate as *Mandata Quilombo* in order to draw attention to her major purpose: focusing on gender and race, by turning the noun *mandato* (Portuguese for "mandate") into its female form, *mandata*. Available at: https://catracalivre.com.br/cidadania/erica-malunguinho-e-a-mandata-quilombo-da-1a-deputada-trans/. Accessed Aug. 10, 2024.

[58] Erica Malunguihno is an educator and cultural agitator. With a Masters in Aesthetics and History of Art from the University of São Paulo, she became the first trans state deputy elected in Brazil in 2018, with more than 55 thousand votes in the state of São Paulo for PSOL.

[59] Maria Clara Araújo dos Passos is a graduate in Pedagogy from PUC-SP. Dos Passos is currently studying at Especialización y Curso Internacional, in Estudios Afrolatinoamericanos y Caribeños Consejo Latinoamericano de Ciencias Sociales (CLACSO) from Facultad Latinoamericana de Ciencias Sociales (FLACSO Brasil). She holds a Certificate in Afrolatinoamerican Studies from the Instituto de Investigaciones Afrolatinoamericanas at Harvard University, and is a member of NIP: Inanna Center for Research and Investigation of Theories of Gender, Sexualities and Differences.

[60] See Werneck (2009).

May 15, 1992, is considered a political milestone, due to the legal officialization of the first travesti association in Brazil and Latin America: ASTRAL (National Association of Travestis and Liberated People).

The insurgent positioning of Jovanna Baby, Elza Lobão, Josy Silva, Beatriz Senegal, Monique do Bavieur, and Claudia Pierry France, 6 Black travestis, resulted in the Travesti Social Political Movement and its political project, which condensed action and critical reflection for the nation.

The reality of violence, perpetrated by the State and experienced by travestis from all regions of the country during the civil-military dictatorship, and which continued even after the promulgation of the new Federal Constitution in 1988, was collectively thought of as a condition that should be profoundly transformed.

From 1992 onwards, progressive Brazilian fields began to witness a political-pedagogical praxis in which travestis organized and acted as pedagogues in political and social relations[61], mobilizing important lessons that aimed to bring together and train travestis from across the country for sociopolitical action.

The praxis exercised by the Movement not only questioned the way of doing Movement politics, such as the, until then, Brazilian Homosexual Movement, but also how to position travestis—and later transexuals—as sociopolitical subjects committed to democratic construction (Evelina DAGNINO; OLVERA. PANCHIFI, 2006).

Regarding the occupation of political positions, the trajectory of Kátia Tapety, being the first travesti elected to the positions of councilwoman (1992, 1996, and 2000) and vice-mayor (2004) in the small municipality of

---

[61] Nilma Lino Gomes, when discussing the Black Movement and its educational actions, states that Brazilian social movements act as pedagogues in political and social relations. In dialogue with the idea presented by the author, we state here that the Social Political Movement of Travestis and Transsexual Women in Brazil also developed an "educational role" (GOMES, 2017, P. 16) when articulating and training travestis for its national framework.

Colônia/PI, demonstrated to the Movement that, in addition to the possibility of demanding public policies, travestis can be at the forefront of political-institutional processes.

Even though, during the Constituent Assembly, travestis were attributed a sub-citizenship [62], the political-pedagogical praxis, exercised in three waves (COACCI, 2018), highlights the political-cultural tensions and propositions made by the Movement, regarding who and which issues are understood by the traditional left, as intelligible for alternative democracy projects created in Latin America (Sonia ALVAREZ; Evelina DAGNINO; ESCOBAR, 2000).

The criticism that "elections without travestis and transexuals are also a coup," made by Indianare Siqueira,[63] reflects the investment made by travestis and transexual women across the country to occupy positions in political institutions.

According to a survey carried out by the National Association of Travestis and Transexuals for the 2020 election,[64] 293 travestis and transsexuals are democratically competing for positions in majority and

---

[62] João Antônio de Souza Mascarenhas, at the time President of the group Triângulo Rosa from Rio, stated in the National Constituent Assembly that "there would be confusion in society between the homosexual and the travesti, which for the gay movement would be a huge error. There is, according to him, the common homosexual and there is the travesti, who in many cases are prostitutes and end up getting involved in petty theft or drugs" (CÂMARA, 2002, p. 57).

[63] Available at: http://desacato.info/eleicoes-sem-travestis--e-transexuais-tambem-e-golpe-diz-indianare-siqueira-ao-ter--candidatura-negada-pelo-psol-rj/. Last accessed November 1, 2020.

[64] Available at: https://antrabrasil.files.wordpress.com/2020/10/lista-final-23out.pdf. Last accessed November 1, 2020. What draws our attention to the survey carried out by ANTRA for the 2020 election is that 38.5% of travesti and transsexual candidates opted for right-wing parties, including parties that the current President was part of, such as PSC (5 candidacies) and PSL (7 candidacies).

proportional candidacies. Of these, 263 are travestis and transgender women.

Similarly, the political femicide (Renata SOUZA, 2020)[65] that occurred against Marielle Franco on March 14, 2018, months before the election in which the Brazilian extreme right reached the Presidency of Brazil, imposed on the Afro-Brazilian population[66] the duty to resume the maxim announced by the griots Adbias do Nascimento, Benedita da Silva and Lélia Gonzalez: the sociopolitical agency of the Black people built a project for Brazilian society.

Experiences such as the Quilombo de Palmares in Brazil and the Palenque de San Basílio in Colombia show how[67] our people have historically carried out mobilizations and developed political tools with the aim of guaranteeing the construction of a society in which dehumanization, exploitation, and subjugation are not seen as insurmountable conditions. In light of the statement by Lélia Gonzalez (2018, p.37) that "Palmares was the first Brazilian attempt to create a democratic and egalitarian society," the

---

[65] Renata Souza (2020), State Deputy/RJ, states that the murder of Councilor Marielle Franco should be seen as a politica feminicide. Souza states that Marielle's murder must be understood in light of the Councilwoman's own trajectory, as a Black woman who recognized the centrality of race, gender, and class in the production of marginality imposed on Black women. Thus, the murder of Marielle Franco is part of an exponential increase in feminicides in Brazil against Black women, whether they are in their homes or at parliament.

[66] We use the term "Afro-Brazilian" to establish a dialogue with other Afro-Latin American and Afro-Caribbean populations who are also competing for projects in their countries. For an in-depth look at Afro-Latin American political thought, see Frank Guridy and Juliet Hooker (2018).

[67] Paschel (2018) draws our attention to the various mobilizations of enslaved people that took place in Latin America. Quilombos, palenques, and other local denominations are seen as pioneering articulations of Afro-Latin American and Afro-Caribbean populations in the face of colonialism. Among these diverse experiences of cimmaronaje and quilombismo, we highlight the Quilombo de Palmares in Brazil (1595-1695) and the Palenque de San Basílio as territories that express the historical insurgency of the population of African descent in Latin America.

collective investment carried out in Brazil today, in which Black femininities and women asserted themselves as a possible way out for Brazil, objectively refers to the continuity of the work started by our ancestors:

For contemporary Black movements, images of quilombola communities have become representations of utopian projects far removed from the racial hierarchies, exploitation and inequalities characteristic of current societies. Quilombos also served as an ideological inspiration for these activists, and for their political philosophies based on ideas of cimarronaje and quilombismo (PASCHEL, 2018, p. 273 - Translated from Portuguese).

It is by continually referencing quilombos, this territory of affections (Mariléa de ALMEIDA, 2018), that the Black Movement in Brazil has evoked/provoked different actresses and actors, who work in the anti-racist struggle, to dispute public policies and, therefore, projects of society.

It is worth highlighting the importance of Aparelha Luzia, a space for arts, culture, and Black politics. Created in 2016 by Erica Malunguinho, then an educator, artist, and master's student in Aesthetics and Art History.

Aparelha was designated as an "urban quilombo, territory of affection and biome of Black intelligence." Aparelha Luzia, in addition to the materializing and the channeling of the cry of various Black movements in a physical space, asserting itself as a quilombo, became an essential vector of this term in common language, thereby doing justice to Beatriz Nascimento's reflection (1985, p. 41) of: "characterizing the quilombo institution, in its transition to ideological principles, as a form of cultural resistance."

Aparelha is recognized as a Black social technology, a space of mediation for the epistemological turn in debates on race, gender, and sexuality. This fact was/is radically fueled and enhanced by the collective and/or individual public speeches made by the travesti who created this quilombo.

## Calling for Other Milestones

In dialogue with the vision presented by Ângela Figueiredo (2018) when discussing the historic March of Black Women held in 2015, in which different organizations and sociopolitical actors marched together in Brasília, we believe that the positioning of Black lawmakers in Brazil today, in the face of a profound humanitarian crisis, calls for a new civilizational milestone. This was expressed in the 2018 election, in which Talíria Petrone (RJ), Mônica Francisco (RJ), Áurea Carolina (MG), Mônica Seixas (SP), Renata Souza (RJ), Olivia Santana (BA), Dani Monteiro (RJ), Andréia de Jesus (MG), and Jô Cavalcanti (PE) were elected. All were Black women positioned in the anti-racist struggle and occupying parliaments in Brazil.

In this new civilizational milestone, the fight against gender, race, and class oppression—understood for decades by intellectual Black women as inseparable constitutes our theoretical-practical efforts in political institutionality.

Thus, public policies will be designed from this Black feminist epistemic place, and will also have as a priority audience the populations that are victimized on a daily basis by the triad of oppressions (Bell HOOKS, 2019). These populations are the ones who know what it is like to not have decent access to health, housing, education, and food, among other precarious conditions.

It is as part of this historical moment, in the interfaces between the Social Political Movement of Transvestites and Transsexuals and the Black Women Movement, that Mandata Quilombo, led by State Deputy Erica Malunguinho, asserts itself as a political-pedagogical project that produces other political, ethical, and epistemological propositions for Brazilian political culture.

Feeding on the foundations of race and gender, Erica Malunguinho's Mandata Quilombo is made up of Black people, mostly Black women. Black women are in positions such as coordinators, chief of staff, executive secretaries, and political organizers. Among them, three Black travestis who contribute to this political project, one as a deputy and the other two as parliamentary advisors.

Our experiences were marked by exceptions. On the one hand, one of us became the first trans state deputy elected in Brazil in 2018, with more than 55 thousand votes in the state of São Paulo for the PSOL. The other was the first travesti graduate in Pedagogy at the Federal University of Pernambuco in 2015, and who completed her studies at the Pontifical Catholic University of São Paulo in 2020.

The unprecedented things that place us as the first, above all, ought to be seen as denunciations. Denouncements that expose the results of the combination of racism and transphobia, which, according to Bruna Benevides and Sayonara Nogueira (2020), of the 124 murders that occurred in 2019, 82% were committed against Black travestis and transexuals.

It is necessary to reflect on the structural impediments that contribute to the fact that it was only in 2015 and 2018 that the first Black travesti women entered these public spaces, whether on the knowledge latifundia[68] (ARROYO, 2014) or on the political-institutional latifundia.

Just as in 1992, in 2018 it is we, Black travestis, who critically rose up and announced the future, despite the absences and non-existences that were produced.

The nominal victory of Erica Malunguinho, as well as the collective victory of Erika Hilton (SP) and Robeyoncé Lima (PE), represents for Brazil what Boaventura de Sousa Santos called "trends of the future" (SANTOS, 2010, p .118).

---

[68] [E.N.] Also known as haciendas and fazendas, latifundia were large agricultural estates that depended on a combination of wage laborers, tenant farmers and/or enslaved people. They are somewhat similar to a plantation in the U.S. South, though not exactly the same given their different historical, political, economic and social contexts.

## Challenges and Perspectives

On the one hand, challenges are put up, and they are real. Regarding the State of São Paulo, actions such as that of Governor João Doria (SP), of confiscating handouts sent to the State Network just because they discuss gender identity,[69] translate to what we will call here the *institutionalization of transphobia as a government agenda*.

In the Legislative Assembly of São Paulo, this institutionalization of transphobia took place, while male and female deputies impeded the progress of affirmative projects, as was the case with bill 491/2019, which proposed to institutionalize the Transcitizenship Program. Proposed by Erica Malunguinho's Mandata Quilombo, this bill was blocked in the Constitutionality, Justice, and Writing Commission, due to its discussion of merit rather than constitutionality.

On the other hand, projects or actions that are committed to making the lives of trans people more precarious are encouraged and collectively agreed upon, as was the case with the removal of transsexual women from the Dossier proposed by Representative Isa Penna to systematize Government data on feminicide.[70]

Bills such as 346/2019, which seek to ban travestis and transsexuals from high-performance sports games in the State,[71] in which clubs and teams run the risk of being fined, were not only approved by Commissions, but also entered into the regime of urgency for voting and approval.

---

[69] Available at: https://g1.globo.com/sp/sao-paulo/noti-cia/2019/09/03/doria-manda-recolher-livros-de-ciencia-que-fala--sobre-diversidade-sexual-nao-aceitamos-apologia-a-ideologia-de--genero.ghtml. Last accessed November 1, 2020.

[70] Available at: https://www.facebook.com/IsaPennaPsol/photos/aprovado-dossiê-mulher-paulista-na-alesp-nosso-primeiro-proje- to-de-lei-foi-aprov/1190984431096195/. Last accessed November 1, 2020.

[71] Available at: https://www.al.sp.gov.br/noticia/?id=398106. Last accessed November 1, 2020.

Roberta Jucá, Cunha, and Junior (2018) have shown us how the Brazilian Judiciary has institutionalized transphobia through its civil decisions.

Adding other elements, what we are highlighting here is the understanding of an institutionalization, therefore an intentional political action, of transphobia as a government agenda articulated by the Legislative and Executive, through propositions and decisions that directly violate the constitutional guarantee of rights for Brazilian travestis and transsexuals.

Faced with this process that guides public policies, from the perspective of exclusion and the precariousness of the lives of travestis and transsexuals, we will have a brief dialogue with Patricia Hill Collins and her article "Learning from the Outsider Within: The Sociological Significance of Black Feminist Thought" (Aprendendo com a outsider within: a significação sociológica do pensamento feminista negro, 2016) to provide clues, even if only initial ones, regarding the political-epistemological implications of the presence and existence of Black transvestites in political positions.

For Patricia Hill Collins, Black women developed a privileged epistemic perspective by being inserted in spaces where the power dynamics of dominant groups are visible, even though they are routinely positioned as outsiders. The experiences of Black travesti Deputies, Co-Deputies, and Advisors at the time of the extreme right resurgence in Brazil, dialogues with the concept proposed by Hill Collins: we are within the structure, and we have the possibility of analyzing the institutionalization of transphobia from within the Assemblies, thus being able to mobilize a political-epistemological-ethical confrontation with its institutionalization.

A confrontation not only at the level of other proposals that objectively oppose those that are committed to structural transphobia. We are also interested in **tensioning** the dominant narratives about who is or is not recognized as sociopolitical subjects, which necessarily implies a process of self-definition (Patricia Hill COLLINS, 2019). Formerly recognized only as recipients of public policies, travestis and Black women today define themselves as the most capable, most skilled, and most sensible to lead the country. This premise led us to create and coordinate the *Parliamentary Front in Defense of the Rights of LGBTQIA+ People at ALESP*, a political-pedagogical space for dialogue and collaboration between mandates, collectives, entities, and independent activists.

Even though narratives such as "The trans deputy," and not just "The deputy," try to constantly position us in this place of the "Other," the one that does not belong within the institutional space; it is precisely through this privileged epistemic place, which both comprises the margin as the center (bell HOOKS, 2019), that we will bring together elements that will guide propositions that meet the challenges posed by the current humanitarian crisis. At the same time, it is up to Brazilian progressive parties to recognize that, today, the critical contribution of travestis and transsexuals to the alternative democratic projects that are being considered in this territory is essential.

Women's fight against racism and for the recognition of LGBTIphobia as a problem in this country cannot be seen as "if there is time, we will solve this."

Much to the contrary, the demand placed on progressive parties in Brazil is that the elevation of a true Brazilian left will only occur when the parties understand that when we discuss changes in power, we are also talking about an identitarian change of power. After all, it is we— women, Black women, and Black LGBTI+ women—who push the left to the left, as Vilma Reis[72] taught us.

---

[72] Vilma Reis is a sociologist, Black feminist, and a great reference for the Black Women's Movement in Brazil. She played an important role in the General Ombudsman's Office of the Public Defender's Office of the State of Bahia. In an interview with Brasil de Fato, she stated

## Our Steps Will Go Afar[73]

What the future presents to us is the continuity of the paths announced/called for by those who have come before. The steps that will go afar relate to the steps that have brought us here. Therefore, it is necessary to recover and value the trajectories and sociopolitical insurgencies of the trans population and the Black population.

Initiatives such as The Brazilian Black Front (1931) and the National Meetings of Travestis and Transsexuals (1993-2019) make explicit the social and political proposition made by those radically committed to the eradication of structural violence maintained by colonialities (BERNARDINO-COSTA; GROSFOGUEL, 2016).

However, it is worth mentioning how certain distorted representations must be critically analyzed. This is not an essentialist stance, as if just being Black or travesti were enough.

We are not interested in representations without an objective link to the historical struggles of our populations. It is necessary to be grounded and deeply committed to a radical political project to transform Brazilian society, being fully aware of what needs to be done and with gender and race as central issues.

At the same time, it is important to understand how the struggles of progressive camps intertwine. The struggles of the trans population and the

---

that it was necessary to interrupt white hegemony in politics by launching her pre-candidacy for Mayor of Salvador (BA). Available at:

https://www.brasildefato.com.br/2019/12/14/vilma-reis-decidimos-interromper-a-hegemonia-branca-na-politica/. Last accessed September 1, 2025.

[73] [E.N.] The usage of afar here refers to a canonical article by Juerma Werneck about Black Feminist social movements. The title is a play on the words far and afar. Its usage was popularized by Vilma Reis. The article can be found here:

https://books.openedition.org/iheid/pdf/6316 last accessed September 14, 2025

Black population go hand-in-hand, and are in the background of the struggle of the homeless population, against mass incarceration, for a public education of quality, for religious freedom, and for decent housing conditions, among others.

Our political project speaks in the first person, as it is marked by "political self-determination" (CARNEIRO, 2019, p. 320), but it concerns the whole. Beyond individualities, it is about a collectivity. It is for the whole society.

## REFERENCES

ALMEIDA, Mariléa de. **Território de afetos: práticas femininas antirracistas nos quilombos contemporâneos do Rio de Janeiro**. Thesis (Doctorate in History), State University of Campinas, Human, Institute of Philosophy and Human Sciences, 2018.

ALVAREZ, Sonia. E ; DAGNINO, Evelina; ESCOBAR, Arturo. Introdução: o cultural e o político nos movimentos sociais latino-americanos. IN: ALVAREZ, Sonia E.; DAGNINO, Evelina; ESCOBAR, Arturo. **Cultura e política nos movimentos sociais latino-americanos: novas leituras**. Belo Horizonte: Ed UFMG, 2000, p. 15-57.

ARROYO, Miguel G. **Outros Sujeitos, Outras Pedagogias**. 2. ed. Petrópolis, RJ: Vozes, 2014.

BENEVIDES, Bruna G.; NOGUEIRA, Sayonara Naider Bonfim. **Dossiê dos assassinatos e da violência contra travestis e transexuais brasileiras em 2019**. São Paulo: Expressão Popular, ANTRA, IBTE, 2020.

BERNARDINO-COSTA, Joaze; GROSFOGUEL, Ramón. **Decolonialidade e perspectiva negra**. Sociedade e Estado, Brasília, v. 31, n.1, p. 15-24, 2016.

CÂMARA, Cristina. Cidadania e orientação sexual: a trajetória do grupo Triângulo Rosa. In: CÂMARA, Cristina. **Cidadania e orientação** sexual: a trajetória do grupo Triângulo Rosa. Rio de Janeiro: Academia. Avançada, 2002; p. 182-182.

CARNEIRO, Sueli. **Enegrecer o feminismo: a situação da mulher negra na América Latina a partir de uma perspectiva de gênero**. In: Hollanda, Heloisa de Buarque. Pensamento feminista: conceitos fundamentais. 1. Ed. Rio de Janeiro: Bazar do Tempo, 2019; p. 313-323.

COACCI, Thiago. **Conhecimento Precário e Conhecimento Contrapúblico: a coprodução dos conhecimentos e dos movimentos sociais de pessoas trans no Brasil**. Thesis (Doctorate in Political Science), Federal University of Minas Gerais, 2018.

COLLINS, Patricia Hill. **Pensamento feminista negro: conhecimen to, consciência e a política do empoderamento**. Boitempo Editorial, 2019.

COLLINS, Patricia Hill. **Aprendendo com a outsider within: a sig nificação sociológica do pensamento feminista negro**. Sociedade e Estado, v. 31, n. 1, p. 99-127, 2016.

DAGNINO, Evelina; OLIVEIRA, Alberto J; PANFICHI, Aldo. **Para uma outra leitura da disputa pela construção democrática**. In: DAGNINO, Evelina; OLIVEIRA, Alberto J; PANFICHI, Aldo. A disputa pela construção democrática na América Latina. São Paulo: Paz e Terra; Campinas, SP: Unicamp, 2006; p. 13-75.

FIGUEIREDO, Angela. **A Marcha das Mulheres Negras conclama por um novo pacto civilizatório: descolonização das mentes, dos corpos e dos espaços frente às novas faces da colonialidade do poder**. In: BERNARDINO-COSTA, Joaze; MALDONADO-TORRES, Nelson, GROSFOGUEL, Ramón (Orgs.). Decolonialidadeepensamen to afrodiaspórico. 1. ed. Belo Horizonte: Autêntica Editora, 2018; p. 203-223.

GOMES, Nilma Lino Gomes. **O Movimento Negro Educador: saberes construídos nas lutas por emancipação**. Petrópolis, RJ: Vozes, 2017.

GONZALEZ, Lélia. **A mulher negra na sociedade brasileira: uma abordagem político-econômica**. In: GONZALEZ, Lélia. Primavera para as rosas negras: Lélia Gonzalez em primeira pessoa. Diáspora Africana: Editora Filhos da África, 2018; p. 34-54.

GURIDY, Frank A.; HOOKER, Juliet. **Tendências dopensamento político e social afro-latino-americano**. In: FUENTE, Alejandro de la et al. Org. Estudos afro-latino-americanos: uma introdução. 1a ed. Ciudad Autónoma de Buenos Aires: CLACSO, 2018; p. 219-269.

HOOKS, Bell. **Teoria feminista: da margem ao centro**. Editora Perspectiva SA, 2019.

JUCÁ, Roberta Laena Costa; SILVA, Jônatas Isaac Apolônio da Silva; CUNHA JUNIOR, Francisco Gilberto. A institucionalização da transfobia no direito civil brasileiro: uma análise da possibilidade de anu- lação do casamento da pessoa transexual. **Insurgência: revista de direitos e movimentos sociais**, v. 3, p. 171-195, 2017.

NASCIMENTO, Beatriz. O conceito de quilombo e a resistência cultural negra. **Afrodiáspora Magazine**, v. 3, n. 6-7, p. 41-49, 1985.

PASCHEL, Tianna. **Repensando a mobilização negra na América Latina**. In: FUENTE, Alejandro de la et al. Estudos afro-latino-americanos: uma introdução. 1a ed.- Ciudad Autónoma de Buenos Aires: CLACSO, 2018; p. 269-313.

SANTOS, Boaventura de Sousa. Uma sociologia das Ausências e uma Sociologia das Emergências. In: **A gramática do tempo: para uma nova cultura política**. 3. ed. São Paulo: Cortez, 2010b; p. 93-136.

SOUZA, Renata. **Feminicídio Político: um estudo sobre a vida e a morte de Marielles**. Cadernos de Gênero e Diversidade, v.6, n.2, p. 119-133, 2020.

WERNECK, Jurema. **Nossos passos vêm de longe! Movimentos de mulheres negras e estratégias políticas contra o sexismo e o racismo**. Vents d'Est, vents d'Ouest: Mouvements de femmes et féminismes anticoloniaux [en línea]. Genève: Graduate Institute Publications, 2009.

# 6

# DANDARA, MARIELLE, AND THE KILLABILITY POLITICS IN BRAZIL

**Megg Rayara Gomes de Oliveira**[74]
**Translated by Ti Ochoa**

## Introduction

Eleven months separate the brutal murders of the *travesti* Dandara dos Santos and the cowardly murder of the Black city councilor Marielle Franco.

Dandara dos Santos was murdered in Fortaleza on February 15th, 2017, by 12 people, among whom seven were adults and five were teenagers, in a cowardly ritual, which was recorded and shared on social media.

Marielle Franco was shot inside her car, in the central region of Rio de Janeiro, around 9:30 pm on March 18th, 2018, together with her driver, Anderson Gomes.

They didn't know each other, but they carried marks on their bodies that placed them in "human populations judged as disposable or

---

[74] Megg Rayara Gomes de Oliveria is a Black travesti and PhD in Education at the Federal University of Paraná. Dr. Gomes de Oliveira's research focuses on ethnic-racial relations, African and Afro-Brazilian art, and gender and sexual diversity. She is part of the Black social movement and the LGBT movement.

redundant" (Achille MBEMBE, 2012, p. 135), and therefore liable to be murdered.

Confined in the terrain of generic brutality, I agree with the thought that power in post-colonial times takes the form of "necropolitics" (MBEMBE, 2012) due to the fact that it advocates, as a standard, for the death of those who are not able to fit into the manipulative norms (Jaime Alonso CARAVACA-MORERA; Maria Itayra PADILHA, 2018) of white cis heterosexuality. Dandara was killed for being a *travesti*, Marielle for being Black, lesbian, feminist, and a human rights defender.

It is not about examining who Dandara and Marielle were, but about problematizing the value attributed to their lives by capitalist logic, in which transphobia, racism, and lesbophobia can be interpreted from the logic of necropolitics, since the lives of some people are considered more valuable than others. Mbembe (2012) develops the concept of necropolitics based on Michel Foucault's (2005) problematizations about biopower.

Osmundo Pinho (2008), gay, Black, researcher and professor, explains that biopower affects the collective body of populations and is constituted in the power of the administration of collective life in the social body.

Foucault (2005, p. 304) then asks: "How can a power such as this kill, if it is true that its basic function is to improve life, to prolong its duration, to improve its chances, to avoid accidents, and to compensate for failings?"

In this sense, racism, transphobia and lesbophobia come to occupy a strategic role in this process and, thus, highlight the deviations "and negative attributes with the imputation of stigma, coming as a warning to the 'normals' who should stay away from the 'spoiled', 'impure', 'unworthy' and 'deservedly' excluded person from the coexistence of the 'normals'." (Waléria MENEZES, 2002, p. 98).

Racism, transphobia, and lesbophobia have been, and continue to be used to reduce the subjects to which they refer to that which is interpreted as a defect.

Inscribed in a capitalist society that attributes value to human existences through "buying and selling of the workforce at its most fundamental level" (Leomir Cardoso HILÁRIO, 2016, p. 205), people like Dandara and Marielle are considered superfluous and therefore can be naturally excluded. In other words, the political action of death is an adequate political formation for capitalism, including deciding who should and who should not die. The murders of Dandara dos Santos and Marielle Franco followed this logic, even if in different contexts.

## Dandara's Murderers

Dandara was a white travesti, poor, with little schooling, without a formal job or defined profession, and a resident of the peripheral area in Fortaleza.

Her murderers, 12 in total, are Black and, just like the victim, are also poor people with little schooling, without defined professions, who live on the Fortaleza periphery.

There are many points that bring the victim and the murderers together and place them in a situation of extreme exclusion, all subject to the coercive actions of biopower. However, Dandara's gender identity was used to justify her murder because she was of lesser value when compared to normative cisheterosexuality, even if expressed in Black, poor bodies that are also liable to be affected by the politics of killability, that is, necropolitics.

I draw attention to the fact that even hegemonic masculinity is not a fixed attribute. This masculinity is constituted by the contact with the other, demanding that the norms of hierarchization be updated. Therefore, masculinities, Black or white, use whiteness and cisheterosexuality to guarantee an uncontested gender supremacy that operates in the sense of overcoming femininity, be it cis or trans. The permanent search for the maintenance of this supremacy attacks, violates, mutilates, kills... It kills travestis in vulnerable situations like Dandara and women on the rise like Marielle Franco.

## Who Ordered Marielle's Murder?

This question, which does not stop speaking and has an open answer, reveals the necropolitics, as mentioned by Mbembe (2012), in operation within the Brazilian State, which authorizes structural and institutional violence directed at people like Marielle, with the deliberate intention of exterminating them.

Marielle challenged the logic of exclusion and managed, as a Black and lesbian woman resident of the Complexo da Maré in Rio de Janeiro, to graduate in Sociology, become a city councilwoman, and have real possibilities of becoming a senator. Her social and political ascension made her an even bigger target.

Evidently, the surveillance of her body, her actions, and mainly her political positions—since she was the voice of thousands of excluded people fighting for rights—triggered the mechanisms of necropolitics that resulted in her execution.

Investigations point to the involvement of militias formed by former police officers and powerful politicians, which is the reason why the case remains unsolved.

The way in which the case has been conducted reveals a bothersome and compromising slowness, which benefits the ones who ordered and committed the crime and can be understood as a message for those who, like Marielle, dare to challenge the structures of power in the way it presents itself.

Even though her execution happened in the center of Rio de Janeiro, there were no security cameras, inexplicably, that could record any image of the murderers. Besides that, the crime scene was not preserved, which, according to specialists, compromised the forensic work, and it took eight months for the civil police to show a simple sketch of the alleged criminal.

## Some Considerations

Dandara dos Santos and Marielle Franco were bold in constituting themselves as subjects of rights, and they moved, each in their own way and with the tools at their disposal, structures presented as natural and immutable.

The fact of challenging the logic imposed by sexism, racism, classism, and by lesbophobia and transphobia resulted in their murders.

The arrest of Dandara's murderers was only possible due to the dimensions the case took, and it was only authorized, in parts, by the logic of elimination imposed by capitalism and necropolitics, which treats the poorest layers of our society as less important and can, thus, be easily replaced.

They are lives that are valued less and need to be eliminated, be it through death or prison. Even so, something new arises when retelling the murders of travestis and trans women, since, as a rule, regardless of social class or the racialization of the murderers, most of the time, they remain unpunished and rarely go to trial.

The murder of Marielle Franco remains unsolved.

The slowness of the investigations, even in the face of pressure by a big part of Brazilian society, groups that fight for human rights in Brazil and abroad, reveals that their murderers are a part of a segment of society that is seen as deserving of State protection because their lives are the ones that are considered important, even if they commit heinous crimes. It seems that there is a deliberate attempt for the case to be forgotten and to become one more scandalous unsolved murder.

This does not mean that the police do not have the competence to investigate; it seems that these authorities do not have the freedom to do so.

## References

CARAVACA-MORERA, Jaime Alonso; PADILHA, Maria Itayra. **Trans Necropolitics: Dialogues About the Device of Power, Death, and Invisibilization in Contemporary Times.** Available at: https://www.scielo.br/j/tce/a/TYJ397gFMBrfCcdch9JZdtf/?format=pdf&lang=en. Last accessed September 1, 2025.

FOUCAULT, Michel. **Society Must be Defended: Lectures at the College De France (1975-1976).** São Paulo: Martins Fontes, 2005.

HILÁRIO, Leomir Cardoso. **From Biopolitics to Necropolitics: Foucauldian Variations on the Periphery of Capitalism.** Sapere aude, Belo Horizonte, v. 7–n 12, p. 194-210, Jan./June 2016 – ISSN: 2177-6342.

MBEMBE, Achille. **Necropolitics, A Critical Review.** In: GREGOR, Helena Chávez Mac (Org.). Aesthetics and violence: Necropolitics, militarization and mourned lives. Mexico: UNAM-MUAC, 2012, p. 130-139.

MENEZES, Waléria. **Racial Prejudice and its Repercussions in the School Institution.** Revista da Fundação Joaquim Nabuco, n. 147, Aug., 2002. Available at: http://www.fundaj.gov.br. Last accessed September 5, 2005.

PINHO, Osmundo. **Racial Relations and Sexuality.** In: OSMUNDO, Pinho; SANSONE, Livio (Orgs.). Race: new anthropological perspectives. 2. ed. Salvador: EDUFBA, 2008, p. 257-284

# 7

# LIVING IS THE ART AND SCIENCE OF RESISTANCE:
## A CONVERSATION BETWEEN JAQUELINE GOMES DE JESUS AND ROSA LUZ

### Translated by Jess Oliveira

Jaqueline Gomes de Jesus,[75] a scientist, and Rosa Luz,[76] an artist, have many things in common, including being born in Brasília and growing up between the outskirts and the Federal Capital.

---

[75] Jaqueline Gomes de Jesus is Professor in the Department of Psychology at the Federal Institute of Rio de Janeiro (IFRJ) and Permanent Professor in the Graduate Program in History Education (ProfHistória) at the Federal Rural University of Rio de Janeiro (UFRRJ). She is a psychologist with a Masters in Psychology and a PhD in Social Psychology, Work, and Organizations from the University of Brasília (UnB), and completed her post-doctoral studies at the Higher School of Social Sciences and History of the Getúlio Vargas Foundation (CPDOC/FGV). She is the lead researcher at ODARA, an Interdisciplinary Research Group on Culture, Identity, and Diversity (CNPq) and was a Visiting Scholar at Duke University from May-July 2019. She is affiliated with the National History Association (ANPUH), a member of the Brazilian Association of Black Researchers (ABPN), and a member of the Human Rights Commission at the Federal Psychology Council (2020-2022). Jaqueline de Jesus was awarded the Chiquinha Gonzaga Medal (2017) by the Rio de Janeiro City Council, nominated by Councilwoman Marielle Franco. She served as the president of ABEH - Brazilian Association of Homoculture Studies from 2021 to 2023.

[76] Rosa Luz is a visual artist, rapper, and advocate for the human rights of transgender and Black people. As a content creator, she focuses on the intersections of race, class, and gender. In 2018, she was named one of the 10 most influential people in the digital creation market by YOUPIX

Through questions and answers, a self-reflection on the paths of resistance across different generations emerges. A dialogue between Black trans women.

**Jaqueline Gomes de Jesus (JJ)** - Rosa, when and how did you start to see yourself as an artist?

**Rosa Luz (RL)** – Look Jaque, when I was a child, I loved going to the theater and wanted to be an actress. In eighth grade, I understood that to pursue this, I should study Performing Arts, and then life happened... I got myself involved with some left-wing organizations and became part of the Student Union. By that time, I was already writing some poems. So I'd say I began to see myself as an artist at the age of 16, during high school. I felt the need to express something I couldn't speak out loud, and painting helped me in that process. Then, in 2013, I decided to change my major (initially, I wanted to study International Relations) and enrolled in the Theory, Criticism, and History of Art major at the University of Brasília (UnB).

There, at 17, I started producing and researching my own creative process as an artist. I met Ruth Sousa, a professor at UnB and an artist, in the Visual Language Foundations class, and her teaching methodology was crucial for me to start making art in a more objective and serious way.

In fact, it's quite symbolic to be discussing all these issues with you now because back in 2016, during my time at the university, I participated in the occupation of the Centro de Convivência Negra (CCN) [Black

---

Builders. Rosa Luz has completed training courses in partnership with YouTube Space Rio, Creators Boost, Avon Brazil, and the UN Brazil. In 2019, she was invited by the US Embassy to participate in the IVLP - International Visitor Leadership Program. She also took part in the 36th Panorama of Visual Arts at MAM-SP and the Feminist Histories exhibition at MASP in 2019. Her work has been featured in several exhibitions in Brazil and worldwide, including an artistic residency in the United Kingdom. Rosa Luz is a multidisciplinary artist working at the intersection of visual arts and music.

Community Center] at UnB. And it was during that time that I first heard about Professor Jaqueline Gomes de Jesus, a Black trans woman who helped build the Centro de Convivência Negra. Hearing this story was very important to me back then.

**JJ** – I always get emotional when I remember that period of my life. It was powerful to be the first one to be in charge of the Affirmative Action System for Black People at UnB, but also excruciating. I would do it all over again, though. I'm so proud to know that that seed, which was the CCN, has generated so many fruits beyond the time we planted it there, in that little corner... It's a shame that the precise memories of what we experienced back in 2003, and how much we worked during those years, were not well preserved institutionally.

In general, Rosa, I never felt fully recognized in Brasília—and my second husband, João Zacharias, used to tell me that—whether as a psychologist, professor, writer, activist, or administrator. I did so much throughout the years, but I never got as much visibility as other people did. Decades ago, I came to the conclusion that this lack of recognition was due to first, being a Black LGBT person, and then, identifying as a trans woman/travesti.

Being persecuted—including sexually—was a constant in my life, since childhood, so I learned early on how to fight back. However, as sweet as I was, the bitter feeling I've tasted in the midst of the world—and simultaneously isolated from it—in my hometown, led me to the conclusion that I needed a new home in order to better exercise my potential and to get out of that bitterness. Years later, Mãe Carmem, my Yalorixá from Salvador, noticed this stain on my heart and taught me that people are not thankful, but the Orishas fully understand the meaning of gratitude. Her words offered me great relief.

**JJ** – Well, let's move forward. In what ways does being a Black trans/transgender woman manifest in your artistic expression?

**RL** – As an artist, I have been interested in themes such as self-portraiture, performance, music, video, and technology, along with a deep regard to oral traditions and writing as ancestral tools connecting all these forms of expression. In this sense, addressing race or gender is inevitable in my work. Even when they're not in focus, it's common for the media and critics to categorize my art, emphasizing my gender identity and the fact that I am a Black woman.

In my debut EP, "Rosa Maria Codinome Rosa Luz," released in 2017, I worked with the language of rap, drawing from the influence of hip-hop culture, which has shaped my identity since my childhood. This EP means a lot to me. It is a cry for freedom; a reminder to myself that I was alive and could heal through art. It turns out to be a musical journey that addresses both representation and self-affirmation, as well as fundamental struggles against sexism, transphobia, and racism, all of which were crucial for my healing process at that time.

Since then, I have released nine more songs, all within the rap genre, drawing inspiration from boom-bap, funk, grime, trap, lo-fi, R&B, and other electronic music genres.

Currently, I'm producing my second EP, "Deise Ex Machina," with the support of ULTRA – União Libertária de Mulheres Trans e Travestis [Trans Women and Travesti's Libertarian Union]. This support was crucial in enabling me to continue my creative endeavors and cover my living expenses during the ongoing pandemic.

As a visual artist, I've been delving into the realms of performance and self-portraiture, with the markers of race, class, and gender intersecting much of my artistic production and research over the past eight years.

One of my notable works is the self-portrait "E se a arte fosse Travesti?" [What if art was Travesti?], created in 2016 to illustrate an event presented by Tatiana Lionço focusing on travesti artists, with the presence of Aria Rita, Amara Moira (who at the time was launching her book *E se eu fosse Puta?* [What if I Were a Whore?] in Brasília), and myself. This event, alongside my artwork, challenged the exclusion of trans people from the annals of art history, whether in visual arts, music, or literature, as our identities have historically been marginalized in academic settings.

In addition to this piece, I also highlight the performance "Affrontando Ideias" [Affronting Ideas], where I stood for thirty minutes with my exposed breasts at the Rodoviária do Plano Piloto (the main bus station in Brasília). This action sparked a local discourse that speaks volumes about the society we live in, ranging from transphobia to harassment. Created for the film "Chega de Fiu-Fiu," [Enough with Catcalling], this performance displayed the intriguing intersection of artistic mediums through technology, integrating performance, video, and cinema.

Lastly, I want to talk a bit about the project *The Silent Path*, where I embarked on a 15-day vow of silence while donning a wedding dress at the Tanteo artistic residency organized by MilesKM in the United Kingdom. With this performance, I aimed to explore alternative forms of communication beyond speech, emphasizing the body as a medium. The wedding dress, once a symbol of tradition, was recontextualized into everyday life, blurring the boundaries of symbols.

This performance resulted in a series of self-portraits and video performances, which are now available online.

When making art, I believe there is also a political dimension behind all of this. Given the current social landscape, acknowledging the existence of trans women and travestis carries immense political weight, especially considering Brazil's alarming rates of murder of transgender people.

**RL** – I'm so curious about your philosophical view on politics. I mean, as a Ph.D. in Social Psychology, how do you see the relationship between art and politics in shaping a more diverse society?

**JJ** – Since I moved from Brasília to Rio de Janeiro in 2015, I missed the opportunity to witness your artistic blossoming firsthand, but I've been accompanying your work with great pride. I see a lot of myself in you, and, revisiting the theme of my dissatisfaction with how my work was treated, I felt optimistic in seeing that you and your work have been receiving recognition. I believe that the acknowledgment of your art also reflects the amazing progress of the Trans Movement in the Federal District, especially compared to the time when I still lived there.

My coming out as a trans woman around 2009 was quite unique, as I was already a public figure due to my human rights activism and because I was pursuing a Ph.D. in Psychology. This led to coverage from major newspapers in the city like the *Jornal de Brasília* and the *Correio Braziliense*. However, this attention remained largely local. At the same time, there was a noticeable silencing around my trajectory. So obstacles persisted, despite the support within the Institute of Psychology, especially from my advisor, Professor Ana Lúcia Galinkin,

As a Black trans woman psychologist and professor, I got rejected by many institutions while pursuing teaching positions, including one position that referenced a book addressing transphobia, racism, and the biases of academic selection teams, to which I had contributed. Despite teaching at private colleges since 2004, while pursuing my Master's degree, it was only in 2016, unfortunately, years after completing my postdoctoral research at the Escola Superior de Ciências Sociais da Fundação Getúlio Vargas [School of Social Sciences of the Getúlio Vargas Foundation], that I finally got a teaching position as a professor at the Federal Institute of Rio de Janeiro.

I am certain that had I been a white cisgender man, my work would have received more recognition and attention in academic circles.

**JJ**: I'd like to pose you another question: how has the music industry reacted to a Black trans woman who is a singer and an actress?

**RL**: Well, with lots of racism and transphobia! I feel like I should sing a different music style if I wanted any recognition in the Brazilian music industry. On top of being a Black trans woman, I primarily sing rap. And hip-hop culture is still heavily marginalized in Brazil.

So, since I don't fit the mold of a commercial artist and haven't signed any contract with a record label, what is left for me is independent work in collaboration with artists whose works resonate with elements of hip-hop culture. This has led me to collaborate with people from marginalized communities who appreciate and connect with my work.

On one hand, society marginalizes rap. On the other hand, rap artists themselves often perpetuate the marginalization of trans people. Consequently, I've faced the challenge of being solely seen as an artist. But when that happens, the partnership tends to last, and incredible songs tend to be created (like "Brazilian Bitch" and "Thanksgiving," both produced by Beats By Velhot).

In my artistic journey, after five years, I started studying music theory and even produced the instrumentals for some tracks. While it may seem a small feat, studying music production independently has been immensely rewarding for me personally. It's fulfilling a childhood dream that my family couldn't afford.

Now, regarding acting: Honestly, I'm still navigating that realm. Despite participating in the documentary "Chega de Fiu-Fiu" [Enough with Catcalling] and winning acting awards for the short film "Estamos Todos Aqui" [We Are All Here], I'm still hesitant to fully embrace the title of actress.

Recently, I was invited by Globo Studios to attend a Self-Tape workshop. I had a nice experience, although I believe there are other trans women who are more commercially appealing and have milder political stances. Maybe they would be more interested in hiring them. Let's see what the future holds, but I already consider it a significant step to to see television networks like Globo investing in trans actresses and travestis.

**JJ**: The artistic field has historically been more open to trans folks, despite its contradictions and erasures. Let's go back in time a little bit: In the 1960s, during the Military Dictatorship, there was a flourishing of revue theater by travestis, who were applauded on stage but beaten or arrested by the police if they left the theater dressed in feminine attire. And even today, we grapple with the issue of *transfake*[77] (when cisgender people play trans roles), as pointed out by the trans artists' movement. So, we've always been visible, but in what ways?

In academia, we face another form of invisibility. As trans folks, we face the total disregard for our right to education from childhood to adolescence and into adulthood. When a few of us manage to break through the university walls, we are not acknowledged as belonging to this space.

Only one other person and I know about this kind of episode: I met a trans woman who graduated in Biology from UnB back in the 1970s, during the years of military rule. Even with the Dean's Office being occupied by an *interventor*,[78] she received her diploma under the name she identified with,

---

[77] [E.N.] For more information about the term *transfake* and its development within the Brazilian Trans* performance arts scene, please see: Leal, D. T. B. (2021). Gender in danger: Transgender people in performing arts in Brazil. Theatre Research International, 46(3), 398-406. doi: https://doi.org/10.1017/S0307883321000341.

[78] [T.N.] *Interventor*, in Portuguese, means *intervenor*. During the Military Dictatorship in Brazil (1964-1985), the figure of the **interventor** was key to the authoritarian control the regime exerted over state and municipal governments. An interventor was a government-appointed official, typically a military officer or an individual aligned with the military regime,

and subsequently was approved in the civil service selection processes for professorships [concurso público], and got a position in an agricultural research institution. I've never mentioned her before because she preferred to remain not visible as a trans woman, like so many other trans people, given the structural transphobia that harms us.

So, I believe that we will only truly have trans representation in the Brazilian academy when the civil service selection processes for professorships adopts and implement affirmative action, not only for the student body, but also for the selection of trans professors. With more of us in the institutional body, we can more sustainably transform the curricula of all courses.

**JJ**: How can we truly achieve trans representation in Brazilian arts, so that artists are no longer stereotyped because of transphobia?

**RL**: I believe we can achieve effective representation through education by investing in access to training for transgender and non-binary artists. It's crucial for trans people to occupy all production spaces, across all artistic mediums. In cinema, whenever the film aims to portray our experiences, I would like to see films with predominantly trans crews. This principle applies to other artistic mediums as well.

For this to become a reality, cisgender individuals need to understand their own gender identity, as misinformation among cisgender folks often leads to violence against trans people. In terms of politics, I believe that we need public policies and data about our population to ensure long-term health and safety.

---

who replaced elected governors, mayors, or deans when the regime deemed it necessary to maintain political control and enforce its directives. Their primary task was to implement the regime's policies, maintain order, and suppress any form of dissent or opposition to the military dictatorship.

In this regard, I advocate for building a society where trans artists can make a living from their art without having to conform to structures established by cisgender or white supremacy norms. In order to achieve this, we need to reconsider our economic, sociopolitical, and cultural structures.

**JJ**: Your last comment reminds me of when I ran for state deputy in Rio de Janeiro in 2018, following the murder of Marielle Franco, which traumatized us all. It was a very difficult year, with the presidential election of Bolsonaro. It was truly painful. Our campaign was anything but easy, especially because we were at the height of anti-PT sentiment in the country. It was clear that the population didn't fully acknowledge Black women. People said there were too many Black candidates, as if white men didn't, as usual, compose the majority of candidates. In this scenario, we, transgender candidates, weren't heard at all.

I remember one time when I introduced myself to a journalist as a trans woman and outlined the 13 points of my campaign, involving proposals discussed with my support group, about education, health, human rights, the prison system, and socio-educational issues; at the end of my speech, she asked what I would propose for the general population. That is, after hearing the word "trans," it was clear that she didn't hear anything I said for the next five minutes.

In another similar circumstance, I was invited to debate with university students, alongside another candidate, also from the left-wing aisle. Well, a seasoned politician, I would say; a white cis man, older than me, who continuously addressed the audience with remarkable arrogance, claiming he would "allow me" the space to introduce myself properly and share my ideas. As if a Black trans woman couldn't reason and engage in a political debate. He was especially ignoring my background as a professor, my extensive experience in social movements, and knowledge about Brazil, since I've been traveling across the country, and also abroad. Surprisingly, I wouldn't doubt if a significant portion of the audience didn't realize the nonsense of the whole situation, getting to the point of admiring the figure of that gentleman, fitting snugly within the stereotype of the parliamentarians who are usually elected.

**JJ**: Have you noticed differences in how white trans artists and Black trans artists are treated?

**RL**: Yes, I believe that cisgender people treat trans artists who pass as cisgender better. This same bias extends to the bodies of white trans artists and Black trans artists. In recent years, I've observed that white trans artists have an easier time occupying institutional spaces, even when their cisgender passing is less pronounced.

My experience as a light-skinned Black travesti, categorized as *parda* by the Brazilian Institute of Geography and Statistics (IBGE), is completely different: I'm often treated in a hypersexualized manner or marginalized for singing rap. I've also had the misfortune of witnessing white trans artists being racist towards Black women. This was particularly challenging to process, especially when we see white individuals not wanting to acknowledge their racist attitudes.

**RL**: What about you? Have you noticed any difference in treatment involving white trans professors and Black trans professors?

**JJ**: Absolutely! As a light-skinned Black woman, I am likewise often hypersexualized. I won't even get into the sexual violence I experienced in adolescence, which I discuss in my book *Como eu não dancei* [How I Didn't Dance]. I'll focus on more subtle situations in my experience as a professor and researcher. For instance, when a leftist male professor learned that I had published a book based on my Master's thesis—which explored the social representations of enslaved people's liberators in contemporary Brazil—and that my book was published by the same publishing house where he published one of his works, he started commenting with the editor on my gender identity and sharing how he would like to get to know me better (not as an author, but in his bed). I also wonder how many white trans people, who mention my work, are listened to, and I am not! There's privilege in whiteness even within trans identity. Especially now, when much of what we produce through scientific research is popularized on social media, often without due credit. You know that feeling... ingrained in us since childhood, that people disregard what we feel and think because we're Black? It's the same feeling regarding gender identity, even in adulthood. Let's think: How many people care about elderly trans individuals?

You know, I think that my going away from Brasília and moving to Rio de Janeiro helped me to break through that bubble. I guess... Obviously, it wasn't without challenges, but in Rio, I've found greater receptivity to my intellectual production. I've been focusing a lot on research and learning a lot from the dilemmas I face as a professor, who also travels across Brazil, at a campus in the outskirts, i.e., in Baixada Fluminense. Prior to the Covid-19 pandemic, which demanded physical isolation, but not social isolation, as I like to say, since we continued working, albeit virtually.

Interestingly, at this point in my life, I've reversed the trajectory, so to speak: if before it took me an hour and a half to leave my house in the outskirts of Brasília to study at UnB, located in an upmarket area, and another hour and a half to return home. Today, it takes me the same amount of time to leave my apartment in the Zona Sul [upmarket area] to teach my students (the majority of whom are Black women) in Baixada Fluminense [a disadvantaged neighborhood]. This place has truly embraced and acknowledged me as a Psychology Professor at the Federal Institute of Rio de Janeiro, and as a permanent Professor in the Graduate Program in History of Teaching at the Federal Rural University of Rio de Janeiro. I must confess I love it when people say I'm from Baixada, even though I don't live there.

**JJ:** *What about you, Rosa? What challenges do you face in establishing yourself as a singer outside Rio-São Paulo?*

**RL:** Well, I often describe my life as a constant juggling to survive. And here I'm using juggling as a metaphor for the various projects I undertake to make ends meet. Since 2018, I've been living off art and content creation on social media, but it's far from easy, as some might think.

In reality, I'm always budgeting and strategizing how to make my projects financially viable while also paying my bills. For this to work, financial planning is crucial, and I feel like I need to be constantly studying. I know artists from the Rio-São Paulo scene, with commercial work, who receive opportunities by email on a daily basis. They have a team negotiating and deciding the jobs that make sense. For me, the logic is quite different: I often need to take the initiative to pursue clients, as opportunities don't regularly land in my inbox. I don't have a team. I myself apply for grants, I participate in fairs and art shows, and I see co-creation as a strategy for dialogue and a long-term organic growth strategy, among other initiatives to sustain my work.

Additionally, I also advocate for human rights as a communicator. Collaborating with organizations is another way to make projects feasible, especially outside the Rio-São Paulo scene.

Besides all these issues and jobs, I have also worked with some brands. Advertising has been a way in recent years to make myself visible. Despite all this, most of my work and clients are in São Paulo, and often I need to leave the Federal District and go to São Paulo to work. Sometimes, I miss out on opportunities for not being there. So in 2018, I moved to São Paulo in pursuit of better opportunities. However, I returned to the Federal District in 2020 amid the pandemic, because I had no family there. To this day, I still feel the impacts of this decision on my professional life.

A year later, I'm still struggling to survive and cover my expenses. There's nothing to romanticize about my life... You feel me? I must tightly control expenses; I still live in a studio apartment, and last month, I didn't have much money left over... Well, I decided to stop talking about vulnerabilities on social media.

I believe that if I continue living outside Rio-São Paulo, I'll probably need to change professions if I want long-term quality of life. That's one possibility. The second option is to return to São Paulo, a city that embraced me, albeit with its contradictions, in a post-COVID context. Regardless of what happens, I will continue producing art.

**JJ:** Thinking about your return to Brasília, the pros and cons of that decision you had to make, about the hatred you and your artistic production faced, and the need for family proximity during these turbulent times of pandemic and pandemonium (equally an infodemic, through which you became a target because of your art engagement), sometimes I ponder the notion my friend, Professor Berenice Bento, once shared with me. She questioned whether there was a strange "Brasília spell" that affects those who were born or raised there. At the time we had this conversation, she was on the verge of moving from Natal back to the Federal Capital, to teach at UnB.

Initially, I told her I didn't feel it. Today, however, I clearly see that I do feel it; I am undeniably drawn to my homeland, yet I struggle to find my place there as a professor. Well, let's hope cracks will emerge in the hardness of institutions. However, we do not live in happy times, right? In the meantime, I'll keep enjoying Rio de Janeiro, which welcomed me and gave me so much, even two husbands (laughs).

**JJ:** Would you like to add anything else?

**RL**: Sure! I want to thank you for the exchange we had in text. I am an artist influenced by anarchy, radicalism, and post-pornography, who is not always received positively by society. I've faced death threats, and I was also reported for indecent acts at the university, during a performance approved by the same university... You're so inspiring and so special to me. You offered me support in difficult times when I was having morally questionable behavior, given that I come from a place of emotional and financial vulnerability. All this had an impact on my mental health and obviously reflected on my art.

Hailing from Gama-DF and currently living in Santa Maria-DF, a city built alongside the road BR 040 just 28 years ago, I often find myself feeling isolated. So, it's immensely reassuring to connect with other Black trans women, who offer genuine support, who often ask if everything is okay without idolizing you, who treat you like a human being. Perhaps you don't even know this, but you were instrumental in helping me regain my intellectual self-esteem. I am so thankful for that. A big shoutout to our existence.

**JJ**: Long live, Rosa! Long live! You know how much I admire you too! You spark hope, not only in the new generations but also in me at 43. You're well aware of everything I've been through—threats, assaults, and other violations that have been normalized over time... Yet I keep smiling because of talents like yours, talents that reverberate far beyond the local scene, resonating globally despite all the pain. As you always say, everything is ours! Thank you. Axé! I'll see you soon!

Rosa Luz in Santa Maria/DF and Jaqueline Gomes de Jesus in Rio de Janeiro, in the first semester of 2021, were still resisting the "syndemic" (confluence of pandemics) resulting from the arrival of COVID-19 in Brazil at the worst possible social and political moment.

# 8

# THE BODY:
## THE DISABLED TRAVESTI

**Luana Rayalla**[79]
**Translated by Ale Mujica Rodriguez**

What does it mean to be beautiful? Do you think you are beautiful? Do you think I am beautiful? Is your travesti neighbor beautiful? Is your disabled neighbor beautiful? Is your fat teacher beautiful? Is your skinny classmate friend beautiful? Anyway, I could talk about all kinds of bodies here, but the truth is that "being beautiful" has been one of the mysteries that our society has always tried to figure out. Furthermore, the definition of beauty has become a political tool, in which a certain group first defines what is beautiful and then, through a well-armed strategy, disseminates it to the whole of society, through the media, as a standard to be followed. Thus, controlling our bodies is a true dictatorship. With this background, how does society view the body of a travesti with a disability?

Today, there are two debates about beauty: the objective and the subjective. The subjective argues that beauty is not in bodies: beauty is in the eyes that contemplate it. This is contrary to the certainty that the Greeks had: beauty is an objective fact. Subjective beauty was leveraged in modernity when

---

[79] Human rights activist, specifically for people with disabilities and the trans community. Library studies student. I love books and geek culture.

all eyes turned to aesthetics, where beauty is what makes you feel pleasant when you look at it. Based on this idea, we should have a very diverse idea of beauty—an immense diversity of points of view to say what is beautiful.

However, that is not how things work, because if you compare my body and appearance with those of other trans women, like Gabriela Loran, Glamour Garcia, Mandy Candy, or Thiessa, you will realize that the issue of being beautiful weighs heavily on trans reality. And the body of a trans person with a disability suffers even more. This is because there is a connection between beauty and "being passable" in trans reality, through certain standards that society determines and imposes on trans women in order to pass the "faith-femininity test." Through this established model, society says that yes, there is an objective trans beauty. However, for a trans person with a disability, depending on their disability, there isn't even the possibility to face, like other sisters of mine, this cruel saga for passability. If being a trans person is not a choice, being a trans person with a disability is living the non-distinction. Because this person will always have to face the possibility of double rejection.

In the text before this one, I said that I flagellated myself for a long time thanks to the cis dictatorship. Because if you, as a cis woman, feel pressured to look for a certain beauty, thanks to pressure from the media and society, imagine trans women. This is where I suffered a lot because I had to deal with the idea that I did not have a "desirable" body, not just for one reason, but also for two reasons: not having the imposed cis beauty and because of my disabled body. I had to deal with two types of body asymmetry. Apart from the social and personal pressures, I suffered putting on industrial silicone to "alleviate" this difference a little; however, I think I have always been good at contemplation.

I soon got rid of this bad idea and accepted my body as it is and learned to love it. I would very much like to share a reflection by Leandrinha Du Art, a disabled woman, which defines and adds to the debate that is being highlighted here:

Hey, trans community, look at the provocation there! What you call DYSPHORIA is what people with disabilities live with every day and are forced to deal with their crooked arms, strange fingers, different voice, this is my case. Different from wearing a thong or not, having breasts or not, having a beard or not, having a penis/vagina or not, which can be "solved," obviously understanding the social factor of access to these changes, we don't have the option of modifying our bodies to make them less disabled. So, "dysphoria" is much broader than what is discussed around in the same intonation of just discomfort. We are conditioned to deal with this discomfort because there is no other option, or rather, there is, which is to hide, complain, and suffer for having been born in a body that is really uncomfortable. Let's understand places of privilege within the little boat called oppression.[80]

Objective beauty, which comes from the Greeks, says that beauty will be revealed over time. For example, when I heard a certain song for the first time, I did not like it, but when I listened to it several times, I began to like it, I began to admire it, and I began to find it beautiful. It has also happened that I found someone who is aesthetically uninteresting, but over time, I have come to find the opposite. This means that beauty is objective—that is, it is in the object or body—but only over time will you discover it. When will it be time to find the bodies of people with disabilities beautiful?

Through experience, I came to understand what the philosophers meant by beauty that awakens feeling. However, perhaps it is a great philosophical paradox that I live in, since I unfortunately paid too much attention at first to the bad feelings that my body aroused, such as pity and repulsion. Which led me to get stuck in the idea of objective beauty, waiting for the time to come when my body wouldn't arouse these terrible feelings.

---

[80] From Leandrinha Du Art's Instagram account, January 18th, 2019. Available at: https://www.instagram.com/leandrinhadu/.

Do you realize that this objective beauty was for a second person to perceive? (Not that I lived according to other people's opinions.) However, it was the opposite; I was the one who was trapped in this torture for a long time, thanks to the cis dictatorship.

When I decided that I wanted my body to be free of the rules set by others, I realized that my body aroused good feelings, such as pleasure and desire. For years, I forgot to let one of the most beautiful things a human being can show shine through: inner beauty. I do not mean to brag, but I managed to make out with many men that way (laughs). That is how I learned what the phrase, "If you obey all the rules, you end up missing out on the fun," that some attribute to Bob Marley and others to Katharine Hepburn, meant.

Regardless of whether or not your body awakens good feelings in someone else, allow that same body to awaken good feelings in you. You will soon realize that if you are secure within yourself, no one can hold you back. I am still deconstructing myself from many things, but I believe I have worked out a good path. How about you?[81]

---

[81] This article was originally published Jan. 23, 2020 on author Luana Rayalla's personal page on the Medium platform. Available at: https://medium.com/@luanarayalla/o-corpo-a-travesti-com-defici%C3%AAncia-592a5a54d29b. Last accessed July 21, 2021.

# PART II
# EPISTEMIC DISSONANCE:
## THE VOICES OF BLACK TRAVESTIS AND TRANS WOMEN IN SOCIAL MEDIA

# 9

# CIS'COLONIALITY AND THE TRANSPHOBIA IMAGINARY

**Thiffany Odara**
**Translated by Ale Mujica Rodriguez**[82]

The process of sociability takes place collectively, taking the singular into the plural universe without losing sight of subjectivity: self to other. In other words, this process happens through connections that differ, or not, in their existence over other forms of existence. Therefore, we can analyze these experiences in a broad way, how we behave, and what we often judge as valuable or not valuable. From this point on, I will make a brief reflection on the existence of travestis and trans people.

How do you see yourself in the world? What gives you pleasure and happiness? In your reality, how many trans people do you know personally? How many trans people have you lived with? Do you know what transphobia is? These are guiding questions for thinking about CIS'COLONIALITY as a mechanism of domination, fed by a racist, capitalist, and patriarchal order that kills trans people on a daily basis.

---

[82] Thiffany Odara is a pedagogue, specialist in gender, race/ethnicity and sexuality, social educator, harm reductionist, and activist in the Black and LGBT movements.

In the light of this brief reflection, I am going to give you a broad explanation, starting from the social position I occupy: after all, the person writing here is a Black travesti. Therefore, I invite you to reflect with me. So let's go!

Trans people are often not seen as humans, so they are not seen as subjects of rights, with the right to life, or access to public health policies. We have little compared to the cisgender model of existence. Has anyone ever stopped you in the street to ask if you really are cis or to say that you do not even look like a real cis man/woman? These commonplace words insist on haunting us. Now, imagine, from where do these questions come? Well, from the cisgender model of being in the world.

Have you ever stopped to think that trans people are also worthy of affection and respect? Most are expelled from their homes simply because of who they are. This is a worrying fact, because there is no effective public policy for this population, which lives on the margins of society. Welfare policies do not take an intersectional approach to analyzing how social markers are intrinsically relevant to social inequalities.

Still along these lines of effect, I bring up the process of compulsory expulsion that takes place in the school environment because of differences. The denial extended by religious temples is a real device that conditions the social imaginary to believe that we are not worthy of affection and family recognition, as seen in the media with Thamy Miranda[83] and recurring in

---

[83] [T.N.] Thammy Miranda, a white Brazilian transman, politician and son of singer and dancer Gretchen, was the first trans man elected to the São Paulo City Council He was elected in 2020 with 43,321 votes, representing the Liberal Party (PL), a far-right political party. Currently, he's affiliated with the Social Democratic Party (PSD). Thammy's gender transition and public life have been widely covered in Brazilian media, partly due to his famous mother and his own career in entertainment. He transitioned publicly in 2014. He faced a backlash after participating in a campaign for Father's Day for the Brazilian multinational Natura with his son, Bento. The controversy led to criticism from some groups, including Silas Malafaia, pastor and leader of the Pentecostal church Assembleia de Deus Vitória em Cristo, who accused him

the lives of many others. This denial is also very prevalent in intimate relationships, where we are often only allowed to have some kind of intimate relationship in the dark and anonymously. It is explicit that this denial of affection permeates areas that are essential to our process of sociability.

Attesting to what was described above, we are thrown into the job market, still being seen from a cis-hetero-patriarchal perspective as a camp for the marginal. According to a survey by the National Association of Travestis and Transsexuals of Brazil (ANTRA), 90% of trans girls and travestis are in prostitution. It is worth pointing out that the vast majority are in prostitution by imposition, and some are not. However, even within this field, we are treated like fetish dolls, there just to satisfy the sexual pleasure of the good-old-bosses of the so-dreamed-of traditional Brazilian family.

This leads to Brazil being the country with the most access to trans porn. At the same time, it leads the ranking of trans murders in the world. According to recent research by ANTRA, in the first eight months of 2020, there was a 70% increase in the murder of trans people compared to the same period last year. Another relevant fact is that the vast majority of those murdered are of the female gender, being travestis and trans women. In other words, the abjection of the female universe is blatant in the face of a cowardly patriarchal society.

"Yellow September"[84] for whom?

---

of promoting an "inversion of values." Thammy Miranda responded by filing a lawsuit against Malafaia for transphobic comments. It's worth noting that Thammy Miranda's family life has also been featured in the media, including his marriage to Andressa Ferreira and the birth of their son, Bento, born via in vitro fertilization in 2020.

[84] In Brazil, September is dedicated to suicide prevention. This campaign began in 2015, aiming to raise awareness of suicide and how to prevent it. World Suicide Prevention Day is celebrated on the 10th of the month. For more information visit: https://www.setembroamarelo.com/.

The data is alarming, given that it is a scenario that gradually reproduces gratuitous violence against trans people. And here we need to reflect: Do trans lives really matter to you? What have you done to show that you really care, given that we still lead the world rankings for trans murders?

Thinking about the social process requires broadening our gaze to other means of sociability and entertainment, of exchanging knowledge that do not reproduce the plastered practices of cisnormativity. It means understanding that social divergence exists because we are different. But when thinking about differences (whether it is gender, race/ethnicity, or sexuality, among others), let them not be seen as marks of exclusion that insist on rescinding and persecuting trans people.

Given the aspects presented here, we can see how coloniality,[85] established by cisnormativity, causes the rotation of a transphobic fantasy in the lives of trans people in an odd way. Here, I will highlight some initial aspects of this debate.

The opportunistic media feels comfortable publicizing trans narratives and creating stereotypes, with which we fall into an imagined common sense, that is, that narrative as the only possible one experienced by trans people. Literally, this narrative serves as a ruler or compass to measure the entire existence of a population, which in itself is diverse. We are seen through a single lens, which leads, once again, to the Cystem formatting us, fitting us into a single way of being in the world. Consequently, this leads cis people to compare us to these characters, who, for the most part, do not talk about our reality.

We need to constantly redefine ourselves every day so that we do not succumb to this norm, and that takes a lot of effort. Wanting to impose that,

---

[85] As quoted by the Programa regional feminismos para América Latina, 2021: "Coloniality is nothing more (in the words of Aníbal Quijano) than a pattern of power that not only took place in one location, but these relations between the modern project that began with colonialism generated a series of racial, social, sexual and geopolitical hierarchies that extend to the rest of the world to the present day."

because you merely believe that we have your approval to exist and to be who you think is best, will not strengthen us at all; remember, we are diverse! No existence should override another; the wounds have no cure, and they are opened daily by this cisgender system of being in the colonial model of determining gender, based on the genital organ that excludes and marginalizes us daily. I do not know if you still remember, but I told you this up there [earlier in this essay].

Society discards and undermines our self-esteem and our bodies, with which we constantly seek passability through the cisgender process—sometimes compulsorily, as a link to protection or even denial.

This anguish makes us believe that nothing is possible, and this is just one of the processes experienced by some. The self-sabotage we often practice is related to the place we are put in and the daily efforts we make to be minimally recognized as humans. Well, we do not want to be mere pets for some local friends who are so-called cis-centered, so that our image can demonstrate that that person or space is legitimized as inclusive. We know how much cisgenderness causes us fear, anguish, affliction, and other feelings, so do not make your imagery our reality, because our reality is marked by the violent inoperability of your cistem.[86]

---

[86] This article was originally published on September 29, 2020 on the blog Notícia Preta. Its publication in this work has been authorized by the author and can be accessed at the following link:

https://noticiapreta.com.br/a-cis-colonialidade-e-a-transfobia-imaginaria/. Last accessed July 21, 2021.

# 10

# CAN A BLACK TRAVESTI WORK IN SOCIAL WORK?

**Jessyka Rodrigues**[87]
**Translated by Flávia Kunsch**

This question has stayed with me throughout my undergraduate studies in Social Service, even IF its Ethical and Political project reaffirms the commitment to confronting discrimination on issues of gender identity, race, social class, ethnicity, and sexual orientation.

The restriction to women's bathrooms and the disrespect for the usage of travestis' social names should draw the attention of professionals who work in defense of human rights and reject authoritarianism. Adopting such positions demands the recognition of ethical responsibilities and the materialization of inclusive action.

---

[87] Jessyka Rodrigues is a Black travesti woman, social worker, and Masters student in Public Policy at the Federal University of Piauí (UFPI). She is a Research Assistant at the Oswaldo Cruz Foundation (FIOCRUZ-PI) and author of the book Sem Rótulos, Por Favor! by Editora Nova Práxis. She is linked to GPTRANS, the Acolhe Trans Group and the National Forum of Black Travestis and Transsexuals (FONATRANS). She is coordinator of the Gender and Sexuality group at NEGRACT/UFDPAR.

These bodies, upon entering the epistemological paradise, destabilize the entire structure, which, until then, had been established as something natural. Automatically, the expulsion mechanisms are activated and legitimized by a cisheteronormative matrix: "This is no place for travestis, go back to the margin!"

Naturalized violence is a dimension that prevents reflection on dissident bodies. This precariousness corroborates our social death.

The feeling of not belonging is constructed from harmful discourses, which feed hardships in connection with society. Estrangement is used as support to inhibit interventions that foster acceptance.

It is well-known that spaces of power, such as education, are forbidden to people who blur the lines of binarism — man, woman. The body that walks through that space is marked by gender and race, categories that are not discussed in Social Work. The (dis)comfort that I caused through my discursive performance was configured as a denunciation of various forms of violence perpetuated against our Black travesti bodies. I have sometimes called for interventions, but the act of not listening is a strategy to maintain white/cis/heteronormativity/Christian/bourgeois privilege.

We only want the right to exist, but after so many attacks, we (re)exist, because giving up is a privilege we do not enjoy. It is not about access; it is more than that; we are talking about the feeling of belonging to a place we can barely enter, of places we have difficulty reaching or cannot remain.[88]

---

[88] This text was originally published March 24, 2021 on Jessyka Rodrigues' personal Instagram profile: @jessyka.rodrigues.37. She authorized its publication in this collection.

# 11

# "BETWEEN US SISTAS":
## FOR AN ABOLITIONIST ANTI-RACIST TRANSFEMINISM

Dora Santana[89]
Translated by Feibriss Ametista Henrique
Meneghelli Cassilhas

Miss Major[90] and my friend Selen[91] do not use the language of Transfeminism; they incarnate abolitionist transfeminism in their attitudes. Just like many of us, within our different fights, but also within our privileges, especially by forcing our presence in elite spaces such as academia, and also by educating, yes, we do, through the language of Transfeminism.

I have chosen to learn/theorize based on conversation, especially those with trans and cis Black women. The dynamics of the conversations vary; sometimes we are right next to each other, laughing, hugging, and saying, "I missed you like crazy!" Sometimes it is rather lonely over there with the text

---

[89] Dora Santana is an assistant professor in Gender and Women's Studies at the University of California, Berkeley. She is a feminist Black trans woman and a storyteller incorporated in flesh and bone, from Maranhão. She is the daughter of Dona Domingas.

[90] Information about Miss Major Griffin-Gracy available at:
https://en.wikipedia.org/wiki/Miss_Major_Griffin-Gracy. Last accessed July 20, 2021.

[91] Information about Selen Ravache available at:
http://tantasnoticiasx1.blogspot.com/2011/08/selen-ravache.html. Last accessed July 20, 2021.

of a companheira[92], as I highlight and write the draft, excited feedback commenting things like, "Yeah! You nailed it, sis!" Dialogical affection between Black women as self/collective care, as a learning practice, is a liberating act in the face of a legacy that imprisons Black and trans bodies.

I was talking to my sista Selen Ravache, sharing the frustration of the violent and lengthy process of legally changing my name when I said, "Sis! There I was standing in front of that psychologist questioning myself, and I knew that was all about a diagnosis!" Selen replies, on the other end of the line, "Dora, and there was I with that judge and all those people in the room questioning you about the change, it felt like you were being judged!"

We shared our frustration in that conversation about the struggle to make them believe our stories. In that case, it is so frustrating going through an invasive and compulsory situation, almost like a confession, to receive a pathologized diagnosis as a condition to have access to basic rights such as legal gender and name recognition.

The feeling of judgment, the feeling of frustration, the feeling of anger, the feeling of anguish, being anxious to act for change—all those feelings were with me. An archive of Black trans women's introspection, in the ephemerality of a telephone conversation. Where else can you find a dialogue archive of Black trans women's introspection if not moments like these? A lot of the effort investing in self-care comes not only from the precautionary measures we take to protect ourselves from a violent situation, but principally in the inner work— coping with anxiety over physical and psychological trauma we have already suffered, as well as the

---

[92] [E.N.] I left the word "companheira" in Portuguese. In the context of this essay, it is being used as the feminine version of "comrade," but comrade does not quite convey the meaning behind the word in this essay. A closer description that conveys the meaning of the world in this context be something like a sister in the struggle. It is a word expressing profound affect and solidarity. Also note that, depending on context, the word can also mean "partner" as in romantic partner, or can be translatable to the feminine version of comrade.

trauma we could still go through. When we arrive alive at home, that does not mean that nothing has happened to us. A whole world occurred inside of us!

The testimony of trans women, especially Black trans women, is always discredited: "Why didn't you react?" "When did you realize what happened?" "What were you wearing?" "Why didn't you run away?" "Why didn't you call the police?" The lack of credibility constitutes a fundamental factor in the denial of basic rights, in which legal processes require a confession, not only in the name change, but also when our bodies are criminalized and imprisoned. Either in a prison of a grotesque and threatening dominant imaginary, or by the imprisonment of our bodies through incarceration. When we are judged in our name change process, we get a feeling that has roots in the same logic that is applied in the judgment and questioning of Black bodies for the purposes of imprisonment. Both processes are punitive in the sense that our womanhood, humanity, the right to live, and the right to freedom are judged and decided by oppressive institutions.

One of those days, I was having an exciting conversation with a text written by Maria Clara Araújo (2016), which considers a highly relevant analysis, based on the radical perspective of Angela Davis, about the necessity to think about the complexity of the category of women. She reminds us that the fight for acknowledging our womanhood is part of the legacy of resistance of Black cis women concerning the category of woman based on white feminism.

Davis (2013) refers to this discussion but highlights the necessity of its intersection with the abolitionist movement against the Prison Industrial Complexes. Davis talks about what abolitionist projects, such as

Transgender, Gender Variant, and Intersex Justice Project (TGIJP)[93], led by Black trans women like Miss Major, can contribute to the thinking about systems of self-responsibility, which can reach beyond the prisons that pile Black bodies, or that kill us in the middle of police searches aiming to incarcerate us.

Miss Major and my friend Selen do not use the language of transfeminism; they incarnate abolitionist transfeminism in their attitudes. Just like many of us, even though we carry on different fights and have different access, especially when we push ourselves, our existences and agendas in elite spaces such as academia. We are also educating, yes, we are, using the language of Transfeminism (just like Hailey Kass and Jaqueline de Jesus, for example). An Anti-racist Abolitionist Transfeminism aims to produce antiracist theories and practices, anti-transphobic, anti-CIS-temic oppression that builds our freedom (as it is enforced by the sista Viviane Vergueiro).

Freedom is our bodily and identity autonomy without compulsory testimony and punishment by being incarcerated. As a Black trans woman immigrant, studying in the country with the highest number of incarcerated Black bodies in the world, a country where trans women and immigrants are criminalized, there is an ongoing anxiety while moving through the streets or participating in protests. The fear of being arrested and deported is constant, and it doesn't disappear along with my resistance in choosing to protest. There are days when "nothing happens," but a whole world happened inside of me.[94]

---

[93] TGI Justice Project is a group of transgender, gender variant, and intersex people inside and outside of prisons and detention centers, raising a family that fights together for freedom and survival. See http://www.tgijp.org.

[94] This article was originally published June 28, 2016 on the Blogueiras Negras website. Its publication in this collection was authorized by Dora Santana. The text in Brazilian Portuguese can be found at:
https://www.academia.edu/26608716/_Conversas_entre_manas_Por_um_Transfeminismo

## References

ARAÚJO, Maria Clara. **Angela Davis e a sua verdade sobre o que é ser radical**. Available at: http://blogueirasnegras.org/ange-la-davis-e-a-sua-verdade-sobre-o-que-e-ser-radical/. Last accessed July 20, 2021.

DAVIS, Angela. **Feminism and Abolition: Theories and Practices for the 21st Century.** Available at: https://www.youtube.com/watch?v=IKb99K3AEaA. Last accessed July 20, 2021.

JESUS, Jaqueline de. **1o Livro sobre Transfeminismo em Língua Portuguesa!** Available at: https://www.geledes.org.br/1o-livro-sobre-transfeminismo-em-lingua-portuguesa/. Last accessed September 1, 2025.

KAAS, Hailey. Available at: http://transfeminismo.com/. Last accessed July 20, 2021.

RAMÍREZ, Boris. **Colonialidad e cis-normatividade. Entrevista con Viviane Vergueiro.** Iberoamérica Social: revista-red de estudios sociales, v. 3, p. 15-21, 2014. Available at: https://dialnet.unirioja.es/descarga/articulo/6624989.pdf. Last accessed September 1, 2025.

_abolicionista_anti_racista_Blogueiras_Negras_?uc-g-sw=73993789. Last accessed September 1, 2025 at 10:11 pm.

# 12

# LGBT REPRESENTATION

Jaqueline Gomes de Jesus[95]
Translated by Feibriss Ametista Henrique Meneghelli Cassilhas

Institutions and political parties insist on the present mistake of thinking that it is possible to grant LGBT representation among them by inviting Drag Queens (only the ones performed by cis gay men) to talk shows to entertain the audience, excluding qualified people who are members of the internal boards of the Movement.

---

[95] Jaqueline Gomes de Jesus is Professor in the Department of Psychology at the Federal Institute of Rio de Janeiro (IFRJ) and Permanent Professor in the Graduate Program in History Education (ProfHistória) at the Federal Rural University of Rio de Janeiro (UFRRJ). She is a psychologist with a Masters in Psychology and a PhD in Social Psychology, Work, and Organizations from the University of Brasília (UnB), and completed her post-doctoral studies at the Higher School of Social Sciences and History of the Getúlio Vargas Foundation (CPDOC/FGV). She is the lead researcher at ODARA, an Interdisciplinary Research Group on Culture, Identity, and Diversity (CNPq) and was a Visiting Scholar at Duke University from May-July 2019. She is affiliated with the National History Association (ANPUH), a member of the Brazilian Association of Black Researchers (ABPN), and a member of the Human Rights Commission at the Federal Psychology Council (2020-2022). Jaqueline de Jesus was awarded the Chiquinha Gonzaga Medal (2017) by the Rio de Janeiro City Council, nominated by Councilwoman Marielle Franco. She served as the president of ABEH - Brazilian Association of Homoculture Studies from 2021 to 2023.

This debate goes far beyond the specific issue of event participation, which is indeed the superficial part of the problem. Beyond the confusion that people create when superficially addressing the topic of representativity, confusing it with representation, which merely reflects the presence of the collective subject's particular cause, in a way that it would never be fully satisfied (someone will always be missing), what matters is to consider the presences and absences in their context, both thematic and institutional.

The limitation of merely symbolic inclusion, fragile because it's not structural, consists in raising visibility for fragments of historically disadvantaged (oppressed) social groups, pleasing the unconscious bias of the dominant group that does not want to see itself as oppressive or unfair.

Superficial concessions do not meet, nor could they ever meet, the needs of the collective. However, they alleviate, even if only temporarily, the guilt felt by those in power, who seek to divert attention from the central issue of discrimination: where are individuals from this group in the structure of the organization itself? How are the members from this group empowered (or not) with their hierarchy? Or are they only remembered on commemorative days?

Regarding groups oppressed because of their gender identity or sexual orientation, the stereotypical idea is perpetuated that their members bring up secondary, inferior, if not laughable, debates. And, for this very reason, they are accessible to these decision-makers, through ridicule, carnivalization, or stereotypical listening, which boils down to only listening to them: when they talk about themselves and even when they talk about the world. In short, they are still treated as a "variation," and their members within the organization as "types," "keychains," in colloquial language, and not as individuals.

This is no longer a fight between the excluded for the crumbs of the included (which perversely amuses them so much that there are high-rated television programs, like Big Brother Brasil, that deal with exactly this; or the fact that networks like Twitter or this one only get a lot of likes through "tretas"⁹⁶). Now the fight is for the banquet. Even if the collective subject is not yet fully aware of this.⁹⁷

---

⁹⁶ *Treta* is a Brazilian slang word meaning "conflict, fight, dispute, polemics.." Its meaning varies according to the context, and in this case it is associated with heated exchange of words and points of view online [T.N.]. This refers to when a topic gains visibility because of the intense level of disagreement.

⁹⁷ This text was originally published on February 10, 2021 on Jaqueline Gomes de Jesus' personal Instagram profile, @instadajaqueline. Gomes de Jesus authorized its publication in this collection.

# 13

# BRAZILIANS OWE A HISTORICAL DEBT TO TRAVESTIS[98]

Maria Clara Araújo dos Passos[99]
Translated by Feibriss Ametista Henrique
Meneghelli Cassilhas

When I looked for some content to help me in the beginning of my gender transition, to my astonishment, I came across an unexpected reality: Brazil was and still is the country with the largest number of travestis and trans

---

[98] This essay was originally written in 2016 and published at the website Blogueiras Negras under the same title. When published, it sparked debates within Brazilian Black feminism on the use of concepts formulated by the Black Movement in essays discussing trans experiences. In brief, it is worth mentioning that this essay was conceived considering encruzilhadas/crossings (ALEXANDER, 2006) between gender and race identities. We took into account the racial-ethnic belonging of the majority of the Brazilian Black travesti population, as well as violence fueled by transphobia and racism combined, a context that reflects in the data that reveals the reality that 80% of travestis and trans woman murdered in Brazil are Black and brown (BENEVIDES; NOGUEIRA, 2021).

[99] Maria Clara Araújo dos Passos is a graduate in Pedagogy from PUC-SP. Dos Passos is currently studying at Especialización y Curso Internacional, in Estudios Afrolatinoamericanos y Caribeños at Consejo Latinoamericano de Ciencias Sociales (CLACSO) at the Facultad Latinoamericana de Ciencias Sociales (FLACSO Brasil). She holds a Certificate in Afrolatinoamerican Studies from the Instituto de Investigaciones Afrolatinoamericanas at Harvard University, and is a member of NIP: Inanna Center for Research and Investigation of Theories of Gender, Sexualities and Differences.

women killed in the world. Unfortunately, half of all those homicides worldwide occur in Brazil. While I was absorbing this information, I started to question myself: why on earth have I not accessed this data before? Why haven't those murders gained visibility on a national level? What has been done to repair the damage? Is this how my life will end?

Just hours before writing this text, sadly, I was once again a victim of transphobia. I still feel the humiliation, but this time I tried to deal with it differently. When I first read the book "Teaching to Transgress: Education as the Practice of Freedom" (HOOKS, 2013), one of the most important extracts, in my opinion, is the one in which bell hooks advises us to theorize our pain. Such a theory has the emancipatory potential to transmute not only its writer, but also its reader, especially those who put this theory into action.

What happened to me today is not an isolated case. On the contrary, it is the everyday life of countless trans women and travestis. In a country such as Brazil, our lives are built on absences, especially when it comes to our rights, the right to live being one of those. Our existence has no value because "we should not exist." That is why we depart from this world in the cruellest ways, as Berenice Bento (2014) has pointed out in her article about transfemicide.

This week, I've heard from a travesti that Brazilians seem to think that travestis do not bleed. With those words, she summarized what I've been living openly as a travesti as well as studying what it means to be travesti in Brazil: "Under Brazilian gazes we are subhuman." Our tears when we are stabbed, our pleadings while we are charred, our cries when we are being beaten... none of that mobilizes them to show us empathy. Once again, our lives do not matter to those who murder us. She does not deserve empathy.

Brazilians, in the process of building their national identity, were taught to feel a strong antipathy for our people, subjugating us as inferior beings. Just like me, you, reading this text, have also listened to specific things about travestis. Insults that create negative archetypes of our identity. However, after my studies, I can refute those lies sold as truth.

When I read "The Mask" (JESUS, 2016; KILOMBA, 2019), a chapter from the book "Plantation Memories" by Grada Kilomba, I could relate its content to the countless situations we are subjugated to: we have a mask on our faces. Travestis cannot talk. Beyond that, even if we did talk, we would not be heard — just as we continue to be ignored every time we try to expose the ills that surround us.

Why are you so afraid to listen to travestis creating their own narratives, that we take control of what is said about us? Reading Kilomba (2019) was a real eye-opener: just like the stereotypes towards Black people are created by whites, stereotypes towards travestis can be seen as a creation of cis people.

Cis people project onto travestis what they have repressed in themselves, making us become what they cannot be and/or cannot get close to, based on their own cis gaze. That is to say that travestis, the "Other," a strange body that has transitioned between the stable and essential categories of our society, becomes what the cis population feels: the fear of being themselves, and disgust in witnessing the Other being themselves.

The problem surrounding the precariousness that surrounds transvestites is in the hands of cisgender people. You owe us a historical debt. Because you have been dehumanizing us and refusing to take a stand against our dehumanization.

If you, cis person, wish to show us empathy, take a firm stand on reparations and start, from this moment on, to change you omissive attitude towards the violence we suffer: create possibilities for our existence, fight for our rights, take care of our physical and psychological health, watch over our paths, ask us if we need something, support us on our journey, and, at last, try to help us and make us feel safe among you.

The greatest commitment that cis people can make to us, the T population, is to repair the historical damage caused by you.

For every cis hand that kills us, there gotta be five to protect us.[100]

## REFERENCES

ALEXANDER, M. Jacqui. **Pedagogies of Crossing: Meditations on Feminism, Sexual Politics, Memory, and the Sacred**. Duke University Press, 2006.

BENEVIDES, Bruna; NOGUEIRA, Sayonara Naider Bonfim. **Dossiê dos assassinatos e da violência contra travestis e transexuais brasileiras em 2020**. São Paulo: Expressão Popular, ANTRA, IBTE, 2021.

BENTO, Berenice. **Brasil: país do transfeminicídio**. Centro Lati- no-americano em sexualidade e direitos humanos (CLAM), 2014.

HOOKS, Bell. **Ensinando a transgredir: a educação como prática da liberdade**. Translated by Marcelo Brandão Cipolla, São Paulo: Editora WMF Martins Fontes, 2013.

JESUS, Jéssica de. **A Máscara**. Cadernos de Literatura em Tradução, n. 16, 2016. Available at: http://www.revistas.usp.br/clt/article/view/115286. Last accessed May 29, 2021.

KILOMBA, Grada. **Memórias da Plantação: episódios de racismo cotidiano**. Translated by Jess Oliveira. Rio de Janeiro: Cobogó, 2019.

---

[100] This article was originally published December 8, 2026 on the Blogueiras Negras website. Its publication in this collection has been authorized by Maria Clara Araújo dos Passos and can be found at the following link: http://blogueirasnegras.org/brasileiros-possuem-uma-divida-historica-com-as-travestis/. Last accessed July 20, 2021.

# 14

# PEDAGOGY OF THE RAZOR BLADE AND MOLOTOV

### Ayra Cristina Sousa Dias[101]
### Translated by Jess Oliveira

Travestis have historically been marginalized, murdered, and raped, even within the movement in which our bodies were tools of revolution. This is why Sylvia Rivera delivered her famous speech "Y'all Better Quiet Down" in 1973, where she denounced the invisibility experienced by travestis[102]

---

[101] Ayra Cristina Sousa Dias is a travesti, Social Work student, poet, drag themonia [monstruous drag performer], mother of the Casa Di Monique, columnist for Geleia Total, and a member of FONATRANS.

[102] [E.N.] In the travesti movement, as in this essay, Sylvia Rivera, and at times Marsha P. Johnson, are referred to as travestis. In consultation with the translators Jess Oliveira and Feibriss Ametista H. M. Cassilhas, we decided to use the gender "travesti" as used in the original text, because the author is making a political claim when claiming Sylvia Rivera as a travesti. This is important for us because this category, at the time of writing this footnote, does not exist as a gender identity in the Anglo-Americas. Thus, the term remains untranslatable. We, of course, hope that this will change, as this term can offer possibilities for people who do not fall under the transgender umbrella but live in solidarity with transgender folks at the intersections of a larger trans* identity. What is important here that like feminism, travesti as a gender and political identity names an experience and a social existence. Feminism did not begin with the coining of the term "feminism," which emerged to name a social phenomenon/experience already in existence, much like the gender travesti She has emerged as a gender identity in Brazil. She exists as a historized subject because Brazilian travestis have undertaken genealogical work to trace her existence. Their work teaches us that she is linked to

within the LGBT movement. Forty-seven years later, the scenario is quite the same; we are still fighting for access to spaces that we historically built.

During a live broadcast on Instagram on April 3, 2020, Lazára Barracuda, an important figure in the Brazilian Ballroom scene, stated: "Transphobia is everything that takes us out of the curve of normality, putting us in the position of the aggressor or the victim." This statement is extremely significant in the sense that, to expose the aggressions we suffer, we need to revisit our wounds, some of which are not even healed. But for those who, in Lazára's words, "will never know what it is like to be in this body," this may seem like an easy task.

We are violently placed in the position of educators, forced to be responsible for the deconstruction processes of everyone around us. Apparently, if we wish to be treated with a little respect, we must play this role. However, this is not a comfortable role for many of us. It is actually hard to smile while giving a painstakingly sweet speech in order to teach the one who just assaulted us to be less of a jerk.

The speech of those willing to play the role of educators is often discredited, even when scientifically grounded. As Florence pointed out in a collaborative live stream with Professor Leticia Carolina on March 30, 2020, "We are always placed in a marginalized position. We are never seen as those who produce science." Thus, cisgender people conceive our speech only as an outcome of our pain. It is important, however, to emphasize that much has been produced to provide theoretical material for society to better

---

a longer historical existence of embodiment dating back to pre-colonial West Africa and the Indigenous Americas. If the category of travesti, as recognized by Brazilians, been an available gender category for Sylvia, would she have embraced that identity? This is a particularly interesting question when we consider that Rivera was also from an Afro-Diasporic Caribbean culture. We leave the term as is, to point an important debate in Brazil, an important debate that can have important implications for countries throughout the Americas and beyond.

understand transgender issues and to help us strengthen ourselves as subjects.

During the same livestream, Leticia Carolina also said, "For us, there is no such thing as passing, we are always killable." This professor's statement is accurate; Brazil has high rates of transgender killings, according to data from the Associação Nacional de Travestis e Transexuais—ANTRA [National Association of Travestis and Transsexuals]. On March 31, 2020, taking an intersectional approach, Sara York shared her life history with Leticia in an emotional talk. She mentioned being 45 years old, having been homeless, and still being alive only because she is white, while her Black travesti friends are all dead.

I am a 23-year-old Black travesti, and I am constantly attacked. The violence towards me is both explicit and undercover. And on top of that, I am constantly attacked for taking a didactic posture; I should apparently empathize with those who harass me. My pain and suffering are not taken into account, but I must consider the process of other people.

Sweet talk appears to have no effect. So, with all that being said, I have adopted what I call the pedagogy of the razor blade and Molotov. That is, I make statements that will be immediately heard, in what is usually understood as a harsh and aggressive way. From now on, I will be bitter and harsh, and whoever expects sweetness can make their own candy at home.[103]

---

[103] This article was originally published April 8, 2020, on Ayra Cristina Sousa Dias' personal Medium site. She authorized its publication in this book. The orginal can be found at: https://medium.com/@ayrasdias/pedagogia-da-navalha-e-molotv-a555e79a7c5. Last accessed September 1, 2025.

# 15

# WHAT DOES IT MEAN TO HAVE SO MANY SOURCES OF OPPRESSION IN A SINGLE BODY DURING THE LOCKDOWN?

Carolina Iara de Oliveira[104]
Translated by Feibriss Ametista Henrique Meneghelli Cassilhas

To be isolated, in quarantine, dealing with the echoes of the present and the past. This must not be only my reality, but the reality of a considerable part of society today, in all its diversity. Well, at least for those who are housed at this moment, who have access to basic sanitation, and are not desperate in the welfare line of the Brazilian Federal Revenue Office to get everything straight with their CPF[105] in order to receive 600 reais from

---

[104] Carolina Iara de Oliveria is an intersex, travesti, posit(h)ive Black woman. She is a social scientist, writer, socialist, and poet. She is Co-Councilwoman of the Feminist Parliamentary Group of PSOL SP, elected with 46,267 votes in a collective Parliamentary Term of Office along with four other women.

[105] [T.N.] CPF is an acronym for Individual Taxpayer Registry. This is a mandatory form of registration for all Brazilians. The numbering is part of a large database managed by the Federal Revenue Service. It is one of the main documents used today in Brazil. [E.N.] In a US American context the CPF has a similar function as a social security number.

the government. Or, there are the rare travestis who do not need to work as streetwalkers downtown or in the periphery,[106] with the very few clients who broke the quarantine because "the president said that everything's ok," so that sex work could provide them with food (yes, I am an exception)."

Well then. Being a Black, intersex travesti person living with HIV/aids, a public employee out on medical leave, I am living with immense contradictions during this coronavirus pandemic, locked in my single-family house inherited from my grandmother, in a peripheral neighborhood called Itaquera on the east side of São Paulo. The same neighborhood that watched me grow up, move to São Mateus (a nearby neighborhood), and return two years ago now sees me locked down, leaving my house every now and then with a cloth face mask, getting straight into the nearest car requested on a ride-sharing application. Or at best, when I have spent all my paycheck, running to the bus stop at a time when I know the buses are less crowded (I did this twice a month, to be precise). I assume, therefore, that I have the right to social isolation, space, and social distancing as prevention. So what?

How is it possible not to go mad with Bolsonaro's eugenics policies, which intend to expose everyone to the coronavirus to see "who is stronger and will boost their immunity," giving the sensation of a huge Nazi

---

[106] [T.N.] In Portuguese, *periferia*. Tiaraju D'Andrea explains that this is a concept that emerged during the Cold War to designate countries under the influence of the world powers of the time, the USA and USSR. But, in an urban environment, the *periferia* or periphery is more than a geographic issue. It is a region with specific social characteristics, often represented by the difficulty in accessing public services or access to only poor-quality services when available, the amount of time it takes to get to the city centers, the higher level of poverty, and the higher level of violence. Besides that, the periphery becomes a certain subjectivity, which is a particular way of seeing the world. This subjectivity is shared by many residents of the Brazilian periphery who perceive themselves as such. Available at: https://periferiaemmovimento.com.br/dificuldades-geram-identidade-periferica/. Last accessed Sept. 9, 2024.

concentration camp in the open air, available for the experiments of the Joseph Mengeles of our day? How could a person not completely lose their mind after seeing COVID-19 deaths on the rise, realizing that people from the periphery are the ones dying at a higher rate at the beginning of the pandemic in São Paulo? Things haven't been easy…

I must share intimacies, since this text aims to share a personal experience. What does it mean to be a Black intersex person, to start with? A person is crosscut by the influence of the biological into the ideological, according to Kabengele Munanga, when he defines race. This can also be applied to my biological identity/condition: being intersex is growing up in between sexes, even when you undergo multiple surgeries, forced hormone therapy, and male socialization. My family has also been deceived by ICDs (International Classification of Diseases) and technical terms, which are difficult to understand, to hide my "level" of intersexuality (back then, it was not even understood or categorized as such). Even then, I always had a sense of nonplace, of nonbelonging to the gender identity I was assigned right after I was born and which materialized using a scalpel on a surgical table.

It has been shown to me that I have not dealt properly with this sense of nonplace as I thought I had in the middle of a heavy schedule, and several means of escapism (alcohol and sex with crushes and also with strangers), but now they have escaped my hands just like a virus through people's noses, through droplets of saliva.

With four months of hormone therapy acting on my body, I am having contradictory emotions, feelings of joy, filling my body with an old desire, the desire for "feminization," and at the same time problematizing, from the perspective of Carol the social scientist, what is feminine, what is masculine, and if all this makes sense at all… The pleasure of seeing the breast nipples swelling, my waist getting smaller, but also the pain of who I could not be, ghosts from the past, genital surgeries, the uncertainty about which surgery I should undergo now, if it is worth it at all, if everything doesn't get smaller in the face of the virus, in front of an asthma inhaler and, again, the virus... though not the HIV virus now, but the so-called coronavirus.

These days, I have been reading about Waris Dirie, the famous Somali model who was a victim of genital mutilation (of the clitoris) in her childhood, something very common in Somalia. I noticed how the newspapers emphasize this as savage, truly evil, and anti-Western; however, in our own backyard, mutilations are performed as surgery in about 2% of the population, the intersex people.

Highly evolved, since always, here in western Brazil, we like to point out the arbitrariness in other people's backyards. In ours, we call those who speak of such "ideological manipulations of the biological," to quote Munanga once more, VICTIMS. Of course, when a 6-year-old child cries in a hospital, when she is having stitches removed after a genital surgery to get her closer and closer to matching a biological sex, regardless of her lack of belonging to that sex, in addition to being told by the doctor to stop crying and ACT LIKE A MAN, it must be something unexceptional, there is no need to note this down, isn't that right?

Just like Waris Dirie, I am a woman, a fragmented travesti. Mutilated. And being quarantined is to be unarmed, naked in front of the mirror, with each estrogen pill taken to "reverse" the body's "masculinization" imposed on me during my childhood, it always comes to my mind the thought of the things I lost, of what I could have been. In vain, obviously. The intersex person's dysphoria is caused by something that will never return, that which is never going to be but was born. And there are no words to express such a feeling. And a few hours after the hormone pill, here come the antiretrovirals,[107] here come the AIDS "jelly beans." Bang, with the

---

[107] [T.N.] In Portuguese, *jujuba* is slang for HIV antiretroviral medicines. The word literally translates to English as "jelly beans."

antiretrovirals, there is another worry: How long will the distribution of anti-HIV drugs continue to be guaranteed by the government, given the imminent collapse of the SUS,[108] which has been encouraged by the president? Is there a possibility that the money used to pay for my medicines will be allocated to COVID aid?

There are so many uncertainties. The rope tightens itself, and we are walking on top of it, trying constantly to keep our balance. And sometimes we pussyfoot around. Some nights, the skin I inhabit breaks into a cold sweat. I feel like a body that has been supervised from a very early age, under the tutelage of specialists, technicians, medicines, probes, artificially constructed penises, asthma pumps, exams, and medical reports... A contradictory relationship between the pleasure and pain of hacking and, often, fighting for such supervision to continue staying alive, being Black, working class, travesti, intersex, posit(H)IVe. But one must keep the balance to turn the game around...

As an antidote, I am inspired by remembering other struggles. I read the news from Folha de São Paulo, or the special collaboration between Universa – a special platform aimed at women from UOL, and Neon Cunha, a Black, South Amerindian[109], transgender woman who is an independent activist – in which she narrates the time she went to court to ask for her name to be changed on a legal document; if the they refused to grant her this right, she would request an assisted death be provided by the State. The same State that mutilates us, that fragments us and kills, trans, intersex, Indigenous, and Black people, will either give us the right to our

---

[108] [T.N.] Brazil's Unified Health System (Sistema Único de Saúde) provides free, universal access to medical care to anyone legally living in the country.

[109] [T.N.] In Portuguese: *Amerindia*. In English, *Amerindian* is defined as Indigenous people from North America. Politically, we refuse to support the idea that the word "America" is a synonym only for North America.

name or a categorical death and sacrament. Bold but assertive, and always wearing a fraternal smile, with great wisdom. Neon, and all the fights carried on for years by countless travestis, transwomen, associations such as ANTRA, pioneers such as Keyla Simpson, Indianarae Siqueira, Jovanna Baby, Bruna Benvenutti, Roberta Gambine, and so many others... They made my existence as a travesti possible because of their fight, because of our fight.

I feel reinvigorated by them, and seeing my mother, Gisa, here with me, making my afternoons and nights happier. She shows me the orange sunset in the gray city of São Paulo, watching the statement of the Ministry with me; but, right after, she drags me to the kitchen for a hot coffee, a sweet word, light family gossip, so-and-so who is dating someone, the success of someone we hold dear, a video call with Camila, the sister who loves me and also feels jealous of her travesti sister when I go out on the street. She stares at the men who leer at me; sometimes she even raises a stink. Messages from friends, the meetings, and work on the Master's degree continue, as do the political battles and the social movement actions. All that without leaving my home.

In the back of the backyard (yes, my house has the privilege of a quite large backyard), I can see my grandmother Altina's rose bush. She, who has already passed, but whose salmon-colored roses have been firm and strong for twenty years in the backyard, surviving bad weather, the ants' deadly attacks, my two dogs. There, limited to a small space of land, the rose bush takes root and reminds me of the ancestor I called grandmother, or *vovóva*,[110] who cherished me in the most difficult moments of pain and doubt, showing me affection just for affection's sake. And in my imagination, this

---

[110] [T.N.] "Grandmother" in Portuguese is *vovó*, which makes *vovóva* a derivative of *vovó*, akin to "Grandma," or "Nana," or many of the other words of endearment used for "Grandma" used in English.

rose bush expands, spreads the possibilities of the multiple, diverse affective connections that I have and that make me stronger. It goes to Rio Grande do Norte and reaches my soulmate Lily Nascimento, a friend who knows how to guess, far in the northeast, if I'm well or not, or if I am just alright. A misplaced comma, and she knows already.

As well as the struggles. Struggles also move life and make us stronger. To resist during the times of the politics of death is to find these scents, these landscapes, these ephemeral moments of life that give meaning to life. It is to have utopia as a possibility. It's practicing what Gramsci said about the pessimism of the intellect and optimism of the will. It is a mix of pains and delights, of weaknesses and strengths. What we need now is breathing during distress. In fact, breathing, according to Mbembe, is a universal right, and it must be our main agenda, given that the policies of destruction of the Social Estate or the explicitly genocidal policies, such as those of our president, hit precisely at the universal right to breathe. The right to a world where everyone has the right to breathe without the risk of suffocation because they had to break quarantine to make a few bucks to eat.

The combination of the tender and the most loving, along with the heavy, the burdens, and the pain from the present and the past. That is the contradiction that inhabits me and that will make me move forward, to solve what needs to be solved, but I know that we will not move forward alone. We need these rose bushes, the solidarity networks, the friendships, the collectives, and the activist comrades. We also need a mirror (or our own reflection) to keep going. And we will keep on moving. It won't be our Nero, or the new minister of the Pseudo-Fourth Reich, the so-called Teich, who will stop us, even after thousands of deaths and tears. After 520 years of resisting, we must have learned something useful from our malungos[111]

---

[111] [T.N.] Professor Jerome Branche provides us with a detailed explanation of the term malungo: "Among the Bantu peoples of Central and East Africa, particularly among the

ancestors crowded together on slave ships (another million dead), from the quilombolas[112] and left-wing working-class rioters (left-wing practitioners of macumba[113]—those who are practitioners of African religion will get it).

Walking towards a utopia of freedom, ample and complete, to quote Angela Davis, that emancipates everyone, is what has moved me for years and what continues to move me, along with the overwhelming desire for life

---

speakers of Kikongo, Umbundu, and Kimbundu, there exists a word, concept in which at least three ideas intersect and combine depending on place and time coordinates The ideas are (i) of kinship or brotherhood/ sisterhood, (ii) of a big canoe, and (iii) of misfortune. The word that brings these concepts together is *malungo*, and for the Bantu speakers who made the Middle Passage, it meant shipmate. In colonial Brazil, the term *meu malungo* referred to "my comrade-with-whom-I-shared-the-misfortune-ofthe-big- canoe -that-crossed-the-ocean." (Slenes, 1995). Because the notion of the ocean (kalunga in Bakongo, another Bantu tongue) is embedded in the idea of a voyage in a big boat, and also refers to the line of demarcation between life and death, *malungo*, for Bantu speakers in Africa, also referred to the "traveler," paraphrasing Robert Slenes, "on the sea of death who came back to the land of the living." (Slenes, 1995, pp. 9-11)." Source: BRANCHE, Jerome. *The poetics and politics of diaspora: transatlantic musings*. New York: Routledge, 2015.

[112] [T.N.] People who live in quilombos. In this collective article published by the Brazilian Association of Black Researchers (ABPN) they define quilombos: "During the Latin American period of slavery (1490-1888), communities were founded by run-away or by abandoned former slaves in rural or jungle areas. These populations are tied to slavery resistance and are known by different names in different countries, such as quilombos in Brazil, cumbes in Venezuela, palenques in Cuba and Colombia, marrons in Jamaica, bush negroes in Suriname, and cimaronaje in Cuba and Puerto Rico. These terms may be equivalent to quilombo, meaning the pursuit of freedom, rebellion and resistance against oppression or run-away slaves (Gomes, 2015; Florentino and Amantino, 2012). [...] The Black Movement from the 1960's-1970's, together with academic representatives, began a political and ideological struggle to unmask racism in Brazilian society, and to show racial differences in socioeconomic and demographic contexts (Popolo et al., 2011) and to repair a historical debt of Brazilian society with the descendants of slaves. [...] In this moment, 'quilombo' was associated to a form of mobilization and struggle for freedom and citizenship, as well as for political, economic and social liberation (Leite, 2015)." Source: PAIVA, Sabrina Guimarães, et al. Migration in Brazilian afro-descendants communities: a new approach to illustrate the meaning of contemporary quilombo. Revista da ABPN • v.12, nº 32 • março – maio 2020, p.188-208. DOI 10.31418/2177-2770.2020.

[113] In this context, *macumba* refers to practitioners of African religion in Brazil.

in me, seeing the orange sunsets more often and feeling people's affection, seeing their smiles and seeing my own smile in the mirror more often. Take a breath as deep as the right to live. I am alive because of all that, because of me, and because of all of us. That's why I'm alive for this, for me and for us! And when this coronavirus situation is all over, I want public displays of affection and a festival of huge hugs.[114]

---

[114] This essay was originally published April 17, 2020, on Carolina Iara de Oliveira's personal Medium platform. Its publication in this work was authorized by de Oliveria. The essay in Brazilian Portuguese can be found at: https://medium.com/@carolinaiaradeoliveira/o-que-%C3%A9-ter-tantas-opress%C3%B5es--num-corpo-s%C3%B3-na-quarantena-3b5de59f2476. Last accessed July 21, 2021.

# 16

# TRAVESTI IDENTITY:
## LANGUAGE DISPUTE AND REDEFINITION

### Dandara Maria Americano da Silva[115]
### Translated by Jess Oliveira

What is a travesti, or rather, what can a travesti do?!

To be a Brazilian transfeminine person means you must have heard the following question many times: "What's the difference between trans and travesti?"

Well, I think it's time for us to instead ask ourselves: "What's the similarity between trans and travesti?" The need to understand what sets us apart speaks volumes about a process of sanitization and construction of social imaginaries, which tends to always marginalize travestis.

Being a travesti in Brazil is about gender, gender expression, class, concept & politics. A travesti can be the whole of an existence in which one is neither a woman nor a man, but a travesti... A travesti can also be a part of a given existence, as in the case of transgender women who understand the sociopolitical weight of also reaffirming themselves as travestis in Brazil. In this case, one's political identity is as important as one's gender identity.

---

[115] Dandara Maria Americano da Silva is a Black travesti lesbian woman, poet, marginal writer, and digital content creator who focuses on race, gender, and sexuality.

"Not every travesti is a trans woman, but every trans woman is a travesti." Any Latin American and especially Brazilian transfeminine person is subject to being read and proclaimed socially as a travesti. Some of us, understanding this context, appropriate the term travesti, stressing it as a gender identity itself. Others, even if they do not exclusively understand themselves as travestis but comprehend the social place they occupy, appropriate the expression, fixing it as a political identity.

A travesti can be a *she*, but not a *he*; a travesti can be a woman, but not a man; a travesti can be trans, but not cis! Just like transgender women, travestis experience their feminine gender through transgenderness, and therefore already face several uncommon situations. Travestis can also experience dysphoria, can have their gender reassigned, can have a family, and can have formal jobs... Just like transgender individuals, they may not have had these experiences.

We have much more in common than uncommon, and we need to overcome this discussion that focuses on our differences, because Brazil continues to lead the world when it comes to killing its trans population, especially Black transgender women. When we are killed, it does not matter if we are women or travestis.

Travestis can do anything, and we are everything we can be.[116]

---

[116] This essay was originally published June 10, 2021 on the author's personal Instagram profile, @afro-transfeminista. Last accessed July 21, 2021. Da Silva authorized its publication in this book.

# 17

# THE CHALLENGE OF BEING A TRAVESTI TEACHER UNDER THE BOLSONARO GOVERNMENT

Ana Flor Fernandes Rodrigues
Translated by Kenai dos Santos Roriz
and Nathalia Amaya Borges

Since I felt the urge to write the essay "What if your son's teacher was a travesti?" as I have been reflecting on the challenges that are being (and will be) imposed during the Bolsonaro government in Brazil. The big impacts are already affecting LGBTQIA+ and the education field, which was already expected, if we consider how neoliberalism and its spawn work.

To start this discussion, I would like to mention that I am beginning to build a teaching identity. As a seventh-semester undergraduate student of Pedagogy at the Federal University of Pernambuco (UFPE), I have been thinking about new pedagogical practices that will enable travestis in teaching; however, this also causes conflicts when we analyze our current situation. It is undeniable that Brazilian politics intervenes and affects the lives of teachers, schools, and students. It also exerts its influence on the teaching and learning process, which we try our best to develop, considering the impossibilities of the Bolsonaro government and its persistent threats.

Currently, in the Pedagogy curriculum at UFPE, there are compulsory subjects, such as internships in schools. In these moments — as well as others — it is possible to establish exchanges with the schools, the teachers, and the students. That way, we are able to build bridges that provide a better understanding of the school's educational practices. Being a travesti who is also a teacher allows me to reflect on some things, and I would like to share these reflections with you.

One of the most renowned authors in the educational field, Guacira Lopes Louro, discusses the rules and regulations placed on bodies that are considered "dissidents" in schools in her famous book "O corpo educado" ("The educated body"). Among these, the travesti identity and body are included. The presence of a travesti student in an institution such as a school has always caused displacements and disruptions in a place that historically promotes exclusion. Then what happens when these same travestis go back to these spaces/places, but as teachers? That is my case.

The debate about gender ideology has caused mass hysteria in the Brazilian population, causing irreversible damage to the LGBTQIA+ population, especially to those of us who work in the educational field. The words "doutrina, kit gay, mamadeira de piroca"[117] – which can be literally translated as "doctrine, gay kit and baby bottles with penis-shaped teats" – were used to censor the work of teachers who envisioned an education that is public and of high quality. Consequently, the right-wing (mis)

---

[117] [T.N.] Those words refer to a series of fake news spread by far-right figures to promote Anti-LGBTI+ School Policies at schools aiming to defeat left winged parties especially during the presidential elections of 2018. According to their fake news, students were being indoctrinated at schools, gay kits and baby bottles with penis-shaped teats were distributed at schools by the Workers Party (PT). What Jair Bolsonaro who was a federal deputy in 2011 referred to as a "gay kit," was the Schools without Homophobia program which provide subsidies to teachers with pedagogical material to address the issues of homophobia within the school system. The distribution of the material was cancelled after protests accused the program of promoting free sex and homosexuality.

government has reverberated its punitive tendencies and scams, affecting a very specific public.

To think on the political interferences regarding travesti identity, in this moment, is to comprehend that the issues involving us, too, are political. A travesti "cannot" be a professor in Brazil because the State, along with an associated camp of institutions, has created a transphobic project in which there are no other possibilities for life in this world. Which means: If travestis are able to create mechanisms and strategies to bypass these techniques, they will be labeled as a great danger. For everything that is not cis is trans and travesti, and what that means, at least for now, is an escape from hegemonic control.

That being said, one of the escape plans (or confrontation plans, depending on one's perspective) is to ensure that more travestis migrate to educational fields. This, without a doubt, is a war tactic that needs to be widely used in Brazil. Guaranteeing the inclusion of travestis in universities must be set as a goal for the next 5 years. To change the route, the path of travestis in Brazilian history is to write other possible worldviews. I have been gleefully calling this project "travesti prosperity." And with that, I don't mean to imply that things will be fixed, but rather that it will bring forth hypotheses to combat the technologies that harm us and that make our bodies more docile and murderable. Not only our bodies, but also our work as teachers.

Lastly, allow me to reiterate that Bolsonaro's governmental plan strives to break up travesti lives, along with public education. Therefore, to think about alternatives and the creation of an education in which cisgender thought is not the center, is to dismantle policies that insist on domesticating us, yet forgetting the tricks and talents of travestis, even while demanding from us the most absurd outcome: marginalization and oblivion. In other words, take care of yourselves—we can be much more than that which the Brazilian social imaginary projects.[118]

---

[118] This essay was originally published February 14, 2019 on Ana Flor Fernandes' personal Medium platform. Its inclusion in this collection was authorized by Fernandes, and it can be accessed at: https://medium.com/@anaflorfernandesrodrigues/o-desafio-de-ser-uma-professora-travesti--frente-o-governo-bolsonaro-bdb0b959080e. Last accessed July 21, 2021.

# 18

# TRANSPHOBIA IS STRUCTURAL AND OUR CHILDREN ARE TAUGHT TO EXPLOIT HATRED

### Dália Celeste[119]
### Translated by Flávia Kunsch

Imagine asking to go to the bathroom and being stabbed to death, being at the bus station and being burned alive, or asking for directions and having your face deformed. Trans women and travestis were killed like this in a span of 20 days. These cases are not just about numbers; they are people with a story, dreams that will never be fulfilled, families in mourning. These are crimes that represent a culture of extermination of these bodies.

On June 18, Kalyndra Selva Guedes Nogueira da Hora, a 26-year-old Black trans woman, was found dead inside her home in the Ipsep neighborhood of Recife. She was the victim of asphyxiation, and her partner is the main suspect. Kalyndra was an artist and performed at many events in the city's nightlife, always holding demanding shows and bringing art as

---

[119] Dália Celeste is an Afrotransfeminist from the favela, and a psychology and criminology student, researcher of gender, race, sexuality politics and law enforcement. A member of FONATRANS.

resistance. She was very active in LGBTQIA+ spaces. The performer, who brought joy to so many lives, had her life brutally cut short by transfemicide.

Less than a week later, on the 24th, the travesti Roberta da Silva, 32, was set on fire alive at Cais de Santa Rita, one of the busiest terminals in downtown Recife. She suffered 40% burns to her body. Roberta was a Black travesti living on the streets and was sleeping when she was attacked by a teenager. Due to the severity of her burns, she had both of her arms amputated and spent a few days in Hospital da Restauração. Unfortunately, Roberta could not resist and passed away on the morning of July 9th of this month. Her death, caused by a teenager, makes us understand that we live in a transphobic structure that teaches children and adolescents how to direct their hatred towards travestis and trans people.

At the beginning of July, on the 5th, Black travesti Crismilly Pérola was murdered with a gunshot to the head in the Beira Rio Community, in Várzea, Recife. Known as Piu Piu, Crismilly was a hairdresser and well-liked in the neighborhood where she lived. Before she was killed, she was beaten up. She told her mother that she had always been insulted in the middle of the street.

In Santa Cruz do Capibaribe, in the countryside of Pernambuco, Fabiana da Silva Lucas, aged 30, was murdered in the early hours of July 7th. The victim asked for directions to go to the bathroom when a man followed her and stabbed her to death. Fabiana was found dead on the banks of the PE-160 highway, with parts of her clothes torn; she was violently attacked without the possibility of defending herself.

Since childhood, trans and travesti bodies are placed in a position of dehumanization and inequality, thus reproducing the belief of hatred and extermination. The man who kills a trans or travesti woman does not kill her out of shame for the desire for this body; he kills because he does not know how to deal with the desire for a body that he has been taught to hate since childhood.

And, in just over 20 days, there were four deaths and five attempted transfemicides in the State of Pernambuco. Last year, the state was the seventh most dangerous place for travestis and trans women to live, according to ANTRA.

On the same day of Roberta's death, while we were still feeling the pain of her departure, the travesti and nurse Fernanda Falcão, aged 28, suffered an attempted transfemicide, inside her own home, in the city of Paulista, Metropolitan Region of Recife.

"Four men arrived on two motorcycles. One of them came up my stairs with a gun in his hand and kicked my door, which didn't give way. People from my street came to intervene for me, but he ran down and left. I spent the whole night at the police station, where I filed a complaint. I got support from an entity that welcomed me and placed me in a safe place. I am hiding. I believe it was a reprisal because I have no problem with anyone, nor any disagreement with anyone. I'm very well-liked in my community," she reports.

This attack made Fernanda decide to go to court with a request for assisted death. She wants to take medicine to die without pain. "It's because of the feeling and the certainty that I'm going to die suddenly. The certainty that my mother will be able to see my body, at least clean, in a coffin, so that I don't have the displeasure of my family catching me in the middle of the woods, in the middle of the street, all stabbed. It's about having dignity at least at this moment," she explained in a conversation with Jornal do Comércio.

Fernanda is a great activist in favor of trans and travesti women in the state, consultant to the State Human Rights Council, the State Committee for the Prevention of Human Trafficking, and the State Mechanism to Combat Torture. She is the coordinator of the National Network of Travestis and Transsexuals and Trans Men Living and Dealing with HIV.

She is active in the Mercador de Ilusões Project, which helps sex workers. Even occupying these spaces, nothing guarantees safety for her life.

Public security policies are needed for this population: measures of inclusion in social spaces, carried out in a humanized way, to reduce the damage caused by trans and travesti bodies being pushed into spaces of marginalization and execution. This is urgent.

Mandates and social movements in Recife, Olinda, and Paulista have put forward requests for specific public policies for the LGBTQIA+ community. Recife City Hall also created a notice for Casa de Acolhida, named after Roberta Silva. Even though this measure is important—which is a great achievement for social movements and activists in the State—it is necessary to establish a dialogue with this population in a more focused manner.

It is necessary for the State and the government to take responsibility for the deaths of trans and travesti people. Structural transphobia denies us spaces for employability, education, emotional and social bonds, love, and affection. This is a problem that is not our responsibility. Cisgender people need to take accountability for the process of extermination and exclusion of our bodies.[120]

---

[120] This essay was originally published July 15, 2021 on the Rede de Observatórios da Segurança's website. Its publication in this collection was authorized by Celeste, and it can be found at: http://observatoriosseguranca.com.br/a-transfobia--e-estrutural-e-nossas-criancas-sao-ensinadas-a-instrumentalizar--o-odio/. Last accessed July 2, 2021.

# 19

# THE STRESSFUL PLACE OF THE BLACK TRAVESTI WHO PRODUCES ACADEMIC KNOWLEDGE

Carolina Iara de Oliveira[121]
Translated by Aline Silva Santos and
Kenai dos Santos Roriz

The academy is mentally sickening, but the field of public health has managed to get even sicker. Unconvinced? Take a look at my testimony, which I will write in second person in order to put you in my shoes: you, Black travesti, social scientist, who spends years studying sociology, anthropology, and public health in a structural, sociocultural sense, are admitted to a fucking Master's program, having to scientifically account for what you do to the thesis advisor, the academic community, to the organizers of compilations. You, who will pass your thesis defense, who must do a thousand complementary activities, etc., etc... at the same time, you go through a gender transition, taking hormones, freaking out about

---

[121] Carolina Iara de Oliveria is an intersex, travesti, posit(h)ive Black woman. She is a social scientist, writer, socialist, and poet. She is Co-Councilwoman of the Feminist Parliamentary Group of PSOL SP, elected with 46,267 votes in a collective Parliamentary Term of Office along with four other women.

facial hair and doing laser hair removal (that, yes, hurts a lot), starting the process of changing documents and such and such...

So you, an anthropologist and sociologist who sells Bach flower remedies[122] and wears "cool" clothing in the minds of many, but in truth wears jeans and little blouses and used to shop at Brás,[123] write an essay analyzing the distance and proximity of AIDS and coronavirus, to analyze the cultural and subjective impact they had on the population, especially the LGBTI+ community. I did as much, in a text I wrote for Esquerda Online (a digital left-wing newspaper), as well as publishing it on my Medium (links at the end). In this same essay, I advance a critique of the belief that people living with HIV are "doing swell" during the coronavirus epidemic, simply for the lack of robust biomedical studies on the interaction of both viruses on the human body... and I close the essay with the discussion of political measures I consider to be of great importance to preserve our lives, the positive lives...

Well then. There comes a so-and-so, white, male, cis, CENTRIST, with a photo of a white apron, tells me that "you ~DO NOT PRODUCE SCIENCE~," that you only produce activism. "I want to know about science, not politics," says the positivist centrist. "I want to know of the vulnerabilities of those who live with HIV, not of activism, he proceeds. Right in the text where I constantly list out the social vulnerabilities that need to be analyzed... and be acted upon. He's not the first, nor the last. I

---

[122] [E.N.] Bach Flower remedies are flower essence remedies used to support emotional balance. Originally created by the British Dr. Edward Bach, his work has been continued around the world by other herbalists. In countries like Brazil, where herbalists have taken into consideration the benefits of Indigenous flowers within a Brazilian context. Now Bach flower essence remedies address a broad spectrum of issues that affect emotional balance and wellbeing.

[123] [T.N.] This is a popular neighborhood in the State of São Paulo, Brazil where people can buy clothes, toys, technological products, etc. Goods sold in Brás are low in price.

have a great list of times where my work as a social scientist and activist has been delegitimized.

Look... I don't know whether to laugh or to cry about the limited notion of science that these people have. This person probably hasn't ever heard of epistemology, philosophy, critique of pure reason, materialist dialectics, none of that. But they overshadow me to reduce me to a non-scientist. If this person did hear about these ideas, they didn't pay attention, bc this person was so anxious to get the "true science." The hard sciences, not even knowing that this term came from the machismo of Positivist Science (this, bc I haven't even begun to talk about its racism.)

But it is not new that a left-wing Black woman, yet a Black travesti, is taken for granted because of the science that she produces, and is tagged as an activist (Lelia Gonzales already talked about this in the 80s). After all, only neutrality could produce science, right? But the thing is, in general, those who are sitting on the fence are truly on the fence's owner's side. The sad part is to know that, in the end, I may have been invited to go to the Pan American Health Organization (PAHO) in Brasilia, I may have been given a prize for activism, I can be in a Master's degree program, I can do a thousand laser procedures on my face and take hormones, but I am STILL a Black travesti. And a communist, to really screw with it all.

SO, WELL. If there is a thing that the coronavirus is showing us about health and biomedical science, it is that collective health, the public health, is interdisciplinary; it involves a variety of sciences, and it involves, also, look at that—POLITICS AND THE WORKFORCE. Everybody is worried about their health, but also worried about their jobs and income. It involves a political contest and an epistemological contest. Coronavirus came to show that biomedical answers without a correct policy do not stop a catastrophe. It shows that quarantine is an issue that involves public security, the economy, culture... anyway, when we talk about health, we are talking about the social reproduction of the conditions to live in this world.

Thinking that a social analysis of all of this is not science is a very reductionist thought. I hope coronavirus may open minds—before it is too late.

And you out there, progressivist and such, who are enrolled in a university in medical fields... don't be this kind of professional. It's just because of this model of society and politics that we are living through this unprecedented public health crisis.[124]

---

[124] This article was published April 17, 2020 on Carolina Iara de Oliveira's personal Medium platform. Its publication in this collection was authorized by de Oliveira, the author and it can be found at: https://medium.com/@caro-linaiaradeoliveira/o-estressante-lugar-da-travesti-negra-que-pro-duz-onhecimento-acad%C3%AAmico-253c33bdà865. Last accessed July 21, 2021.

# 20

# AS LONG AS THERE IS STRENGTH IN THIS BLACK TRANSFEMININITY, I WILL GO ON:
## THE CHALLENGES OF A MARKED BODY AND TENSIONS AMIDST THE COVID-19 PANDEMIC IN MY UNDERGRADUATE THESIS

Joane Victória Viana Bastos[125]
Translated by Bruna Barros

Well, I do not know where I should start or where I will end this essay. I think that perhaps this will be documented in history, and it might help many people think outside traditionalist, tacky, and square boxes. Could this essay be a reminder of where we are as a society, reproducing the inequalities and precariousness of life?! I do not want to play the role of a passive victim, a poor thing, nor do I want this to resonate in a predictable and cliché way, or even as some sort of caricature ruined by stereotypes,

---

[125] Joane Victória Viana Bastos is a pedagogue with a degree from UEMG/Unidade Carangola, where she is a social educator, graduate student, and lecturer in Inclusive Education and Diversity. She is Thematic Coordinator at the Instituto Brasileiro Trans de Educação [Brazilian Trans Institute of Education] (IBTE), with an emphasis on race/ethnicity relations. A member of NEAB – Center for African-Brazilian Studies at UEMG/Carangola, Bastos is co-founder of the Coletivo Mulheres Negras Carangola [Carangola Black Women's Collective]. She is a member of the Rede Mineira de Mulheres Negras [Minas Gerais Network of Black Women].

which, for now, sounds like something that represents everyone like me. I must emphasize that we are multiple people, and the experiences I express here are just a part of a whole.

First of all, I understand how important it is to locate myself in order to contextualize this essay. I live in a small town in the countryside of Minas Gerais, Brazil, a town called Carangola, which has 33 thousand inhabitants according to the 2019 IBGE census. Here, I study pedagogy at Minas Gerais State University (UEMG), I am in my last semesters, close to getting my undergraduate degree, and I am writing my undergraduate thesis. The journey I had to venture through until I got to writing this work has demanded many breakthroughs from me, since I first began my Higher Education in 2017, being the first and only trans body in my academic unit, and not simply just a trans body, but a Black trans body.

I remember that, in my first semester, for fear of transphobic retaliation, I had to come out as trans to my anthropology class when the professor was talking about multiculturalism and discussing gender diversity and sexualities. When they are unaware of the fact that we are trans people, uncritical cisgender people believe they should say, "Wow, you do not look like you are trans!" when we tell them. And if that were not enough, we still have to hear: "Wow! You fooled everyone!" as if we were wandering subjects of expression and creation, set out to deceive cis people and make them doubt who we are. Here I explain exactly how we are associated with a lie, or a poorly made caricature of what it means to be who we are.

This is a necessary debate that we need to bring to the core of cis existence, as well as trans existence, given that no one makes such comments questioning the place of cisnormativity, nor is anyone interested in knowing how these technologies of the annihilation of difference stealthily culminate and slowly kill us. I understand that I have the right not to present any data about my subjectivity that is implicitly linked to my being in the world, but since in this town "everyone knows everyone else," at some point my greatest "sin" and "secret" would come to light. So, I choose to face these cisnormative tensions right away and show my face, instead of letting everything run wild, allowing the burden to result in inappropriate and unsustainable situations.

Only we know how painful it is to feel transphobia in the eyes of others, in the cafeteria, hallways, classrooms, auditoriums, offices, and so on. Imagine if all of this also came along with racism?! Well, the Covid-19 pandemic began at a complex and unexpected time for many people. However, for a Black trans woman who experienced an extremely lonely and silencing process of education in elementary, middle, and high school, this moment has been marked above all by ups and downs in my process of writing. It is worth mentioning that, in the last year of my undergraduate course, I ended up becoming mentally ill.

I had already shown some signs of uncontrolled, intermittent, involuntary anxiety, and experienced trouble organizing my ideas in my head by the time I finally and fortunately got a "yes" from a supervisor to work on, and discuss, our marginalized and "marginal" bodies in education.

Some doors closed because I was unable to handle academic opportunities and tasks that would be important for my resume and career. The feeling of this pressure on yourself is very strong, the fear of not being good enough is corrosive.

I remember that a professor, the same one from the anthropology class where I "came out," said to me: "Look, we have very good people here, but you need to be so much more than that! You need to be better than them, even better!" Hearing that affected and scared me at the same time; it made me feel an even greater deal of pressure. I remember that, at the beginning of the 2020 semester before the pandemic, I was feeling mental fatigue.

When my academic life started, my mental health improved; but then soon came the coronavirus and made everything worse! I was so excited and lively; the university faculty was going through a transition. New professors had gotten in through public examinations and were finally starting to work, there were new challenges, adaptations, fears and so on... The viral cycle cut the main bonds of closeness I had made, which had been neglected in my previous education, where I always felt empty and that my professors did not believe in me. I did not receive the same attention as my other colleagues, it was always the same, brutal stereotypes made me have extremely low self-esteem.

The University was clearly not made for our bodies, to the point that it still does not understand our arduous paths to get there. I see this, because it still clearly reproduces its hegemonic white liberal cis heteronormative alignments.

Having all these problems highlighted, felt, and perceived, I see that, although academia reproduces a corporativism of exclusionary relationships — in addition to being more theoretical than practical and inclusive, both in terms of ensuring our permanence there and in terms of having a more cautious look at our bodies within this structure, instead of always placing us only as an object of study and research — it certainly has been a turning point in my journey.

At University I was able to bring up issues that could make transgender people visible and break down some walls, presenting accounts and participating in some debates, projects, activities, and lectures of great social relevance, especially for the vulnerable groups I am part of. The technological computer teaching modality nicknamed "Online Learning," the sort of distance learning offered by the State's current institution, has made it very hard for me to adapt, since I can develop myself much more when I feel the energy and vibration of eye-to-eye interactions with my professors.

For someone like me, who has always been put in a position of invisibility, losing these interactions and exchanges of encouragement was very damaging, to the point that I seriously thought of dropping out three times. I also had anxiety attacks and felt pressured, not to mention the family and financial problems triggered by the Covid-19 crisis. I used to work independently, selling accessories and cosmetics in the places I mostly went to, and taking on cleaning jobs to maintain my monthly income. But now everything has fallen apart due to this whole context. Another source of extreme tension, fear, discomfort, and panic is the fact that, on the street where I live, there is a hospital to which all confirmed cases of Covid-19 are being transferred. Amidst all these crises and struggles, we must not give up on ourselves. As activist Angela Davis says, "Freedom is a constant struggle…"[126]

---

[126] This essay was originally published in the collection "A docência LGBTI+ e a narrativa da escrita acadêmica em tempos de pandemia," edited by Sayonara Naider Bonfim Nogueira and Ti Ochôa Tesser. Instituto Brasileiro Trans de Educação [Brazilian Trans Institute of Education] (IBTE): http://observatoriotrans.org/produ%C3%A7%C3%B5es. Last accessed July 21, 2021. The author gave permission for its publication in this collection.

# 21

# THE PRIVILEGE TO WORK

### Ayra Cristina Sousa Dias[127]
### Translated by Ti Ochoa

I had a childhood full of love, games, and studies, but as a poor child, daughter of fishers from the small town of São Caetano de Odivelas in the country part of Pará state, I also learned the value of work. This was reason for the pride of an entire community that still fights to survive. I was shaped by these values, but today I understand work as a privilege and, not rarely, as a violent process.

At the age of 23, different from when I was 12 or 13 and used to sell manioc cakes on the streets of Odivelas, or when I used to spend afternoons selling *coxinhas* (a fried snack stuffed with pulled chicken) in front of my house, I am prevented from working. My résumé is evaluated, and I am worthy of an interview; however, when I get to the place, I lose the position immediately, as my travesti body screams and bothers a society that does not hesitate to violate us.

---

[127] Ayra Cristina Sousa Dias is a travesti, Social Work undergraduate student, poet, drag themonia, mother of the house Casa Di Monique, columnist at Geleia Total, and a member of FONATRANS.

The violence begins in the act of writing a professional résumé because at this moment, I decide to accept all the violences imposed by the job market, as it's no different from before; working is not an option, it is an obligatory condition to guarantee my survival, as well as those of the ones that are born Black, poor, in peripheral areas, or are gender dissident, as in my case.

Wanderley Santos, Brazilian sociologist, developed the concept of regulated citizenship. He argues that capital and the state develop strategies and norms that workers have to follow to guarantee their status as citizens, because the value of people in societies like ours is given through work. Therefore, travestis, within these processes of violence, also lose their right to citizenship.

On July 8th, 2020, I participated in a job interview; at the end, the interviewer, who was a cis white man, said that some people did not fit the profile and claimed that some were too qualified. I realized he was talking about me because, without false modesty, I had the best résumé of all the interviewees, being the only one with experience in the area of the position applied for.

When leaving the room, I was faced with panicked expressions from the employees there, with looks that, according to my interpretation, said: "Who let a travesti come to this job interview, here?" I left with the certainty that I wouldn't receive a call by the end of the day. However, I received it and the person on the other side said: "Unfortunately, you will not be able to continue with us, good luck on your journey, good night!" in an embarrassed tone.

It's funny to think that, even if I am open to face violence, to die a little every day, to have my existence denied, as even under inhumane conditions, I'm not worthy. It's strange to say that this exploitation process to which many workers are subjected is a privilege, but unfortunately, the formal job market is a space destined for a few people, and many will be expelled only because they exist.

After all, I don't bring myself down, because I knew this all could happen. I will keep trying, hoping that one day I will have the chance to prove I am a skillful professional, committing myself to another process of violence where I will have to work three times more than the others to show my value.

The question at the end of the interview was, "What is your dream?" Now, given everything that happened, I would dare to say that today I dream of a society in which letting myself go through these violences is not an option. I will not forget this day; it will be one more of those **that I use as fuel to destroy this cisheteronormative society.**[128]

---

[128] This article was originally published July 13, 2020 at Geleia Total. Its publication in this book was authorized by Dias, and it can be found at:
https://www.geleiatotal.com.br/2020/07/13/o-privilegio-do-trabalho-por-ayra-dias/. Last accessed September 1, 2025.

# 22

# BLACKTRAVESTIS AND TRANSGENDERS:
## REVERENCE TO STRONG ROOTS

Yara Canta[129]
Translated by Aline Silva Santos and
Nathalia Amaya Borges

When I started to write this column, some ideas came to my mind. However, I believe that the only possible starting point right now is talking about those who came before me. I want to maintain and create new narratives for Black trans people and travestis, and I want these narratives to be based on living and nurturing a different future. To do that, we need to visit the past, which is also the present.

Our great matriarch Jovanna Baby, founder of the Movimento Nacional de Travestis (Nacional Travestis Movement), has been fighting for the civil rights of travestis and trans people since 1979. Jovanna Baby, Elza Lobão, Beatriz Senega, Raquel Barbosa, and Monique Bavier were the first

---

[129] Yara Canta is a multimedia artist from Ceará (Brazil) and an activist for trans and travesti people's rights, especially Black trans and travesti people. is a member of Associação de Travestis e Mulheres Transexuais do Ceará (Atrac)—Travestis and Transgender Women's Associantion from Ceará—and of Fórum Nacional de Travestis e Transexuais Negras e Negros (Fonatras)—Nacional Forum of Travestis and Transgender Black People.

to stand up back then, founding the first NGO for travestis and trans people in Latin America, known as Grupo Astral, in 1992. Today, Jovanna Baby is the president of the National Forum of Black Travestis and Transsexuals (Fonatras), of which I am a proud member. On the forum site, there is a section explaining the history of the social movement for travestis and trans people in Brazil. Additionally, a book detailing the whole story of the social organization of travestis in Brazil will be released soon: Bajubá Odara.

Kátia Tapery is another great precursor of the movement. In 1992, she was the first travesti elected to political office, and we are lucky to have an amazing free documentary about her life online. Another important documentary is about Keila Simpson, who is currently the president of the National Association of Travestis and Transgenders Associação Nacional de Travestis e Transexuais (ANTRA).

And our kinswoman from Ceará, the lovely and unforgettable Thina Rodrigues, who was and will forever be a great name in the movement, cannot go unmentioned. Unfortunately, she left us in June after complications due to the new coronavirus (COVID-19). Thina was the founder of the Associação de Travestis e Mulheres Transexuais do Ceará (Atrac)—Travestis and Transgender Women's Association from Ceará— an institution in which she was the president for many years. She was present in the construction of trans and travesti people's civil rights. I should mention, especially, the right to a social name, which became a city law in Fortaleza in 2017 (Ceará State, Brazil). This is one of the achievements of Thina and of other partners in the movement. Thina Rodrigues will forever be present, and her legacy will never be forgotten.

Their fights and the fights of others that came before us made my existence, and that of many other Black travestis in Brazil, possible. I have special affection for Mel, who is one of the greatest national pioneers in my main field of work (music and art). If today I am the artist, singer, actress, militant travesti, and Black person that I am, it's because I realized that I was not alone. It's because I know that we have been here for a long time, creating new narratives.

We tear apart patterns imposed by whiteness, by the colonial and cissexist system that tries to kill us all the time. We create life! We are the past, the present, and the future. We are the clever ones. We have the strength and the wisdom of all our trans ancestries. We are building a solid future because we have strong roots.[130]

## Documentaries To Watch:

"UM atentado violento ao pudor." Direção: Gilson Goulart e Keila Simpson. Produção: Flavia Teixeira. Realização: Gilson Goulart. Roteiro: Gilson Goulart e Keila Simpson, 2017, 91 min.

"Kátia," directed by Karla Holanda. Synopsis: Kátia Tapety became the first travesti elected to a political position in Brazil. Kátia Tapety was councilor and vice-mayor. Available at: https://www.youtube.com/watch?v=aQok38s7mMA. Accessed July 21, 2021.

---

[130] This article was first published September 10, 2020 on Ceará Criolo's website. Its publication in this book was authorized by Yara Canta. The Portuguese version can be found at: https://cearacriolo.com.br/travestis-e-transexuais-negras--reverencia-as-raizes-fortes/?fbclid=IwAR3iCPp_leGAd5Suyc1X1X---PRL4gVnYCEvc181ugZqZN7ZFMzeL2TQD9b8. Last accessed July 1, 2021.

# 23

# WHAT IS A TRAVESTI AQUILOMBAMENTO CAPABLE OF?

Leticia Carolina Nascimento[131]
Translated by Feibriss Ametista Henrique
Meneghelli Cassilhas and Kukua Dada

As a decolonial family, the travesti aquilombamento can (de)construct family bonds, making us all each other's mothers and daughters.

Beyond blood DNA, what unites us is the *sorrowrity*,[132] in our blood spilled on the streets, in this country with the largest number of travestis killed.

---

[131] Leticia Carolina Nascimento is a Fat, travesti Black woman, Northeasterner, and an Afrodiasporic religious person (Axé person). Pedagogue and Professor at the Federal University of Piauí (UFPI), PhD student in Education (UFPI). She is author of the book Transfeminismo, in the Feminismos Plurais Collection coordinated by Djamila Ribeiro. Linked to NEPEGECI/UFPI; RIMAS/UFRPE; POCs/UFPEL. She is a researcher linked to ABPN and AINPGP. She is a social activist working as co-founder and coordinator of the project Acolhe Trans, and she works alongside the national executive coordinator of FONATRANS.

[132] [T.N.] In Portuguese: *dororidade*. This is a concept from the feminist writer Vilma Piedade, a Brazilian Black cisgender woman. It mixes *sororidade* (sorority) with *dor* (pain, grief or even sorrow). Vilma came up with this concept because the idea of sorority, even though it is an important concept for Feminism, was not enough to describe the Black experience. *Dororidade* takes into consideration the sorrow caused by racism. *Sorrowrity* is our recreation of this term in English.

We reinvented the patriarchal conception of family in the quilombos to protect ourselves from the colonial torturers and executioners.

Like a decolonial school, the travesti quilombo can turn life into a place for building knowledge, breaking down the hierarchy between knowledge and action.

Horizontal conversations become classes, the experience makes each one a master in some contexts, but also the apprentice in another moment, which is why we all teach and learn.

There is no knowledge more important than the other. We learn what makes us live every day, whether it's a makeup tip or how to change our names at the civil registry office. Everything is important if it makes us live.

As a decolonial clinic, the travesti quilombos can heal our wounds, and we are welcomed with an exchange of glances, sensitive listening, friendly words.

As a decolonial shelter, the travesti quilombos can be a place of hospitality, where differences do not inferiorize us.

The simple gathering of our existences is love, learning, healing, and shelter.[133]

---

[133] This essay was originally published October 28, 2020 on Leticia Carolina Nascimento's personal Instagram profile, @profaleticia_ . Its publication in this collection was authorized by Nascimento.

# AFTERWORD:
## DISSONANCE IS LIFE; OR HOW WE MIGHT ALL LIVE QUEER LIVES

### Rinaldo Walcott[134]

That queer life is Black life should be a commonplace assumption. The ongoing demand for queer life that shows up in Black diaspora studies reminds us that Black queer lives remain outside the domain of certain accounts of Black life, still. The epistemic erasure of Black non-heterosexuality and of gender plurality seeks to contain the unruly nature and practices of what it means to live a life. The closure enacted on Black sexuality, and the denial of gender plurality into a binary gender system and a heteronormative account of Black life, are, in part, a kind of self-inflicted violence. Black queer people refuse to participate in this through their affirmative and lived experience of gender and sexual diversity as constitutive of the totality of Blackness. Attempts to study Black queer life in its many complexities, iterations, and presentations are often hampered by those being reduced to a comparative study between a normative white queerness and a singular Black queerness, narrowing the latter to the regimes of racism and exclusion that can neither fully account for Black queer life nor entirely contain it. Black queer life is eruptive, expansive, and capacious both intramurally and extramurally.

---

[134] Rinaldo Walcott is Professor and Chair of Africana and American Studies. He holds the Carl V. Granger Chair in Africana and American Studies. He is a writer and critic. His research is in the areas of Black Diaspora Cultural Studies, gender and sexuality with interests in nations, nationalisms, multiculturalism, policy and education broadly defined.

*Epistemic Dissonance: The Existence of Black Travestis and Trans Women in Brazil* reorients what it means to study Black queer life in the Americas and across the diaspora. These essays provide accounts, testimonies, evidence, conceptual leaps, and intellectual insights that complicate and offer nuanced engagements with exclusion, racism, violence, and the other social factors that shape life to provide a view of those lives from the inside, revealing that the lives being lived are much more than the sum of injuries. The difficult social factors, practices, and evidence of injury are not discarded but rather accorded their place in time as Trans women and Travestis tell the story of their lives, revealing that their existence exceeds the impingement of social categories that they themselves did not author. Instead, we as readers encounter self-authorship across multiple categories of being. The essays and testimonies in Epistemic Dissonance explode numerous categories, such as citizen and woman, to provide not only socio-political accounts of life but also intimate ones, as well as demands for ethical engagement.

When I was a small child coming of age in Barbados, some of the fiercest queer people were people I would now recognize as Trans people. These mostly Trans women lived fully as the gender they understood themselves to be. Those genders sometimes aligned with the normative gender performance of women, and sometimes they did not. What was always clear, though, was that they were refusing the binary system in favor of some other way of being. This was the mid-1970s, and these fierce queer people lived their lives out loud and proud. These acts of living and making a life were not easy, and I have come to understand as an adult queer person that these people insisted on a self-authoring against and in the midst of multiple forms of violent reaction. The toughest among them would fight back, physically and verbally, against the abuse that would often greet them walking the streets of the neighborhoods I came of age in. And yet there too was a grudging acceptance of their existence in those neighborhoods. In fact, some of those, mostly Trans women and at least one Trans man, were well-respected among their peers and others, and children were particularly expected to show them respect. The complicated mix of potential violence, grudging acceptance, and respect produced an atmosphere of at least tolerance in those middle-class places in which whispers of non-heterosexual behavior by apparently straight men were a norm that broke heterosexuality apart even as it simultaneously ruled all of life. Epistemic Dissonance helps us to understand the complicated dynamics of Black diasporic life as it is gendered, sexualized, and racialized.

The authors of the essays in Epistemic Dissonance open up the terrain for thinking Black diaspora sexuality across many domains – from the street to religious practices. What is striking is how Trans women are the foundation of queer visibility, resistance, and rights, as well as the making of queer community. The queer story of my youth is buttressed by the understanding that, in the eventful arrival of AIDS/HIV, it was first Trans women who took it upon themselves to organize to save lives from the catastrophic assault of the illness. From Stonewall to lesser-known queer acts of resistance, we find queer resistance everywhere. Trans people are its foundation, and Epistemic Dissonance demonstrates and confirms this evidence for Brazil most forcefully as well.

Trans women allow us the possibility of exploding the complex dynamics of the category of "woman" in Afrodiasporic formations. Rather than understanding Trans women as some subset of womanhood, we might rather understand womanhood itself as fluid. Indeed, in many Afrodiasporic religious and spiritual practices, the category of woman can expand, contract, and dissolve. Candomblé is one such religion. The various iterations of the Spiritual Baptists, of Voodoo and other African-derived syncretic religions – all of them related in some fashion and through which provide us the evidence, and the experience of how the binary gender system and heterosexual dominance are not the singular reigning categories of life in other realms. Many an Afrodiasporic religion in their ecstatic practices refuse binary gender and heteronormative postures. Epistemic Dissonance leads its readers into the intellectual terrain that allows us to see more clearly what has been sustained despite attempts to silence and erase the fullness of our existence.

The world we are currently living in has sought to make Trans people a problem of life and living. Yet, Trans people exist as persons intent on authoring lives fully, with the experiential knowledge that the body has its own account that it wishes to make present. In essence, Trans people confirm the malleability of our species as not just one thing. Were we all to come fully into our bodies as a species, we might understand the future is Trans. The claim that the future is Trans is not to fetishize Trans people as either an identity or practice, but to assert that in the future, coming to terms with ending the erasure of difference and instead learning to live with the necessary dissonance of sexual diversity and gender plurality might yet free us globally.

# TRANSLATOR BIOS

**Aline Silva Santos** - Brazilian black woman, born and raised in Salvador, Bahia. Mom of 3, proofreader and editorial assistant at Edufba (Federal University of Bahia Publishing House).

Dr. **Ale Mujica** is an anti-colonial trans-feminist and activist. Medical doctor (UNAB - Colombia). Master's and PhD in Collective Health - Federal University of Santa Catarina (UFSC - Brazil). Currently a postdoctoral student in the Interdisciplinary Program in Human Sciences PPGICH-UFSC. Since 2015, I've worked as a translator and reviser, specializing in scientific writing in English, Portuguese, and Spanish.

**Bruna Barros** is a poet, translator, multidisciplinary artist, and researcher. They are currently a graduate student at the Literature and Culture program of the Federal University of Bahia (UFBA), working on the translation of Black Brazilian Portuguese poetry into English. They are half of the cocoruto art duo, a translation-art collective they co-founded with Jess Oliveira.

Dr. **Feibriss Ametista Henrique Meneghelli Cassilhas** is an Assistant Professor of English and African, Afrodiasporic, and Indigenous Inter-transdisciplinary Studies at the Federal University of Bahia (UFBA) since 2019. PHD in Translation Studies, she's been working as a translator since 2007 and is the cofounder of Sarau Vozes Negras (@vozesnegras on Instagram), a Black collective of intersectional poetic-pedagogical practices.

Master in Translation Studies, **Flávia Kunsch** has been a teacher and a translator for 25 years. Her experience varies from English courses to undergrad teaching. As a translator, she has worked with multinational companies, working mainly in industrial construction sites, as well as in literary translation and other media.

Dr. **Jess Oliveira** is Assistant Professor of German and Afrodiasporic Literatures at the Federal University of Bahia (UFBA) and was previously a Visiting Professor in the Department of Spanish and Portuguese at Colorado College. They have translated over 25 books, were a finalist for the 2020 Jabuti Award in Translation, and are co-founders of the cocuruto translation-art duo.

**Kenai Roriz** is a student of the Interdisciplinary Bachelor in Arts at the Federal University of Bahia (UFBA), with focus on Modern Foreign Language studies. He's a Transmasculine, Genderqueer aspiring researcher, artist, and human being.

**Kukua Dada**, aka Karabá Afefé, is a Black trans multiartist and a Pedagogy student at the Federal University of the State of Bahia (UFBA).

**Nathalia Amaya Borges** is a Brazilian researcher, translator, and game localizer. As a language enthusiast, avid reader, and big fan of everything related to literature, working as a linguist has been a dream come true for her.

**Ti Ochoa** Tesser is a travesti from Brazil. She has worked as an English teacher, a translator, and an interpreter for more than a decade. She is also a dancer, an artist, and part of the Brazilian Ballroom Culture.